The Employer's Pa[yroll Question and] Answer Book
(2017 Edition)

Author: Paul E. Love

Copyright 2017 Paul Love

Other titles by the author:
The Business Insurance Question and Answer Book
The UAV Question and Answer Book
Rescue Me: Animals in Need
Find an IT Job
Virtual Robotics: Robotics on a Budget
The Intelligence and Espionage Question and Answer Book
Cowboy Shooting Sports
The Volunteer's Guide

CONTENTS

Introduction

Once upon a time payroll was pretty simple. Figure each employee's gross pay, subtract federal, state and local taxes (and possibly three or four other deductions) and write a check for the net amount. Nothing stays simple for long though -- pretty soon along came direct deposit, 401(k) plans, cafeteria plans, vehicle allowances, the Earned Income Tax Credit, garnishments, third party sick pay, paycards, and a raft of other complications.

For many small companies, payroll went from taking an hour or so each pay period to a process that can consume a whole day or more. And that's just to produce the paychecks -- there are usually various files to be written and reports to be filled out as well.

Unless you have an accountant or a payroll service to handle things payroll can be a very confusing, time-consuming task. For a new employer it can be frustrating just figuring out how to get started; and even employers who've been at it for a while can run into problems when new situations arise or payroll laws change.

The purpose of this book is to give a quick overview of what every employer needs to know about payroll. There are a number of sources of information for employers that can provide more detailed explanations of different topics (IRS Publication 15 or "Circular E" being the most important one). Appendix A lists a few additional sources and many others can be found using internet search engines.

NOTE: The information in this book deals primarily with payroll laws and practices in the United States.

Summary of Payroll Changes for 2017

- The due date for submitting 2016 W-2s and 1099s to the SSA and IRS has changed from the end of February (the end of March if submitting electronically) to the end of January (the same due date for supplying W-2s and 1099s to recipients).
- The deadline for Applicable Large Employers to supply 1095-C forms to their full-time employees (or part-time employees who enrolled in health coverage provided by the employer) and to the IRS has been moved to March 31st, 2017.
- Social Security Rate and Wage Base – The employee rate will remain at 6.2% for 2017, the same as the employer's matching contribution rate. The social security wage base increases to $127,200 for 2017, while the Medicare tax rate stays at 1.45% of taxable wages.
- Again in 2017 individuals who earn $200,000 or more per year in FICA (Social Security and Medicare) taxable wages will have to pay additional Medicare tax. An additional 0.9% must be withheld for Medicare as soon as an employee reaches $200,000 in FICA taxable earnings for the year (for a total Medicare rate of 2.35% instead of the usual 1.45%). Note: the additional Medicare tax does not affect the employer match, which stays at 1.45% for Medicare and 6.2% for Social Security for a total of 7.65% (up to the Social Security wage limit of $127,200, and 1.45% thereafter).
- Employees participating in a 401(k) or 403(b) (or most 457plans) can contribute a maximum of $18,000 for 2017 (unchanged from 2016). For employees who are 50 years old or older the "catch-up" contribution limit stays at $6,000 for 2017 for a maximum annual contribution of $24,000. Note: Even if you don't turn 50 until December 31, 2017 you can still contribute the additional $6.000 catch-up for the year.
- The limit on contributions to either a Traditional or Roth IRA is still $5,500 for 2017 with an additional $1,000 "catch-up" limit for individuals who are age 50 or over.
- The SEP IRA employer contribution limit for 2017 increases to $54,000 or 25% of the employee's salary (up to a maximum salary of $270,000), whichever is smaller.
- For SIMPLE IRA or SIMPLE 401(k) plans the 2017 contribution limit remains $12,500 (with a $15,500 catch-up limit for those who are age 50 or over).

- 2017 Health Savings Account contribution limits are $3,400 for individuals (with a catch-up limit of $4,400 for those 55 and over) and $6,750 for families (with a catch-up limit of $7,750 for those 55 and over). Note: Employer contributions to an HSA need to be reported on the W-2 in Box 12, code W.
- The contribution limit on Flexible Spending Accounts (FSAs) increases to $2,600 for 2017.
- The 2017 maximum tax exclusion for adoption assistance and the maximum adoption credit is $13,570 per child (for individuals with Adjusted Gross Income below $203,540). Employer adoption assistance payments are generally excluded from federal withholding but are subject to Social Security, Medicare and FUTA tax.
- The federal standard mileage rate for business travel is 53.5 cents per mile for 2017, down from 54 cents per mile last year.
- The 2017 monthly limit on the amount that may be excluded from an employee's income for qualified parking benefits stays at $255 per month
- The general definition of a "highly-compensated" employee for 2017 is anyone who receives annual compensation from the business of $120,000. A key employee officer is defined as anyone who receives annual compensation of $175,000 or more.
- Under Affordable Care Act regulations employers with 50 or more full-time or full-time equivalent employees who don't offer affordable health insurance that provides minimum value to their full-time employees and their dependents may be subject to a penalty if one or more full-time employees receive a Premium Tax Credit in the Health Insurance Marketplace. Note: in this case a "full-time" employee is one who works an average of 30 hours per week. Employers with 50 or more full-time and full-time equivalent employees have to offer affordable, minimum essential coverage at minimum value to their full-time employees and their dependents or be subject to penalties. Note: Employers with 100 or more full-time and full-time equivalent employees won't be assessed penalties if they offer acceptable coverage to at least 95% of their employees in 2016.
- Mandatory employer reporting requirements for the Affordable Care Act (Obamacare) went into effect in 2015. Information reporting is similar to Form W-2 reporting in that an information return (Form 1095-B or 1095-C) will need to be prepared for each applicable employee and these returns will be filed with the IRS at the beginning of the next calendar year, with the same filing deadlines as Form W-2. **Note: For 2016 reporting the**

deadline for providing 1095 forms to employees and for filing with the IRS has been moved to March 31$^{st.}$

- Just a reminder – Employers must pay all federal taxes online or by phone using the Electronic Federal Tax Payment System (EFTPS). The only exception is for employers who owe $2500 or less at the end of a quarter – those employers can send their tax payment along with their 941 form (Employer's Quarterly Federal Tax Return) or with their annual 943 or 944 form.

- New Federal Tax Tables – The IRS has issued new withholding tables for 2017 (see IRS Publication 15 for 2017).

- The FUTA (Federal Unemployment Tax Act) tax rate dropped from 6.2% to 6% on July 1, 2011 and will stay at that rate for 2017.

- Employers with 250 or more employees in 2016 are still required to file W-2s electronically using the Social Security's Business Services Online system. You can request a waiver from this requirement by filing Form 8508 with the IRS at least 45 days before the January 31, 2017 due date for filing W-2s with the Social Security Administration..

- Beginning with the 2012 W-2's all employers with 250 or more employees in the preceding year were required to report the total cost of all "applicable employer-sponsored health care coverage" provided to an employee on the employee's W-2 (box 12, code DD). Employers with less than 250 W-2's won't be required to report health care coverage costs until at least 2017. The cost of employer-sponsored coverage is basically the total of employer and employee contributions to any group health care plan made available to an employee that is non-taxable to the employee. Types of coverage excluded from the overall calculation include: coverage under an HRA (Health Reimbursement Arrangement), long-term care coverage, stand-alone vision or dental coverage, contributions to an Archer MSA or Health Savings Account, salary reduction contributions to a health FSA, and any coverage not excludable from gross income. For further details see IRS Notice 2011-28.

- The small business healthcare tax credit (part ot the Affordable Care Act) changed in 2016. Small business employers with 100 or fewer FTEs (Full Time Equivalent employees) are now eligible for a maximum tax credit of 50% of premiums. To claim the tax credit employers must cover at least 50% of the cost of employee-only health care coverage for each employee. To apply for the SHOP (Small business Health insurance Options Program) tax credit employers need to file form 8941. Note: A relatively small number of companies appear to have qualified for the SHOP tax credit according to multiple sources.

- Additional changes go into effect this year in regards to the Patient Protection and Affordable Care Act (see the chapter on the Affordable Care Act).
- At this time the tax treatment of health insurance premiums paid to an employee/owner remains the same for C corporations and S corporations. For C corporations the amount of health insurance premiums paid for or reimbursed to an employee who is also an owner has to be treated as taxable wages for income tax and FICA purposes. For a 2% or more owner in an S corporation the total of the premiums is treated as taxable wages for income tax but not for FICA or FUTA tax.
- Standard U.S. Per Diem amounts for 2017 are $91 per day for lodging and $51 for meals and incidental expenses.
- Note: You can download IRS and SSA forms at any time from www.irs.gov. All downloaded forms can be filed with IRS with the exception of copy A of forms W-2, W-3, W-2C and W-3C – the Social Security Administration only accepts the red ink copies of those forms (or an approved substitute).

Alert – Change in Overtime Rule for Exempt Employees

The Department of Labor has changed the regulation regarding overtime pay for exempt (non-hourly or salaried employees). Currently only exempt employees whose annual salary is less than $23,660 per year are eligible for overtime pay. The new DOL regulations more than double that amount, to $50,440 per year. Under the new standard any exempt employee earning less than $50,440 per year would have to be paid overtime pay for working more than 40 hours per week.

Employers need to be aware of this change and be prepared to keep track of exempt employee hours the same way they keep track of time worked by hourly employees.

NOTE: As of January 2017 a court order has blocked implementation of the new overtime rule – and indications are that the rule may be rescinded or revised.

Getting Started (For New Employers)

Q: **What's First?**
A: Before you do anything else, if you have just started a new business you need to apply to IRS for an Employer Identification Number or EIN. Your EIN identifies your company and appears on every form you send to the federal government. You apply for an EIN by filling out Form SS-4. You can call IRS at (800) 829-4933 and request a form or you can go to the IRS web site (at www.irs.gov) and fill out a Form SS-4 online. You can also obtain an EIN by calling the IRS's Tele-TIN line (1-800-829-4933) which allows you to apply for and receive an EIN over the phone (you still need to fill out an SS-4 and send it in). Once your SS-4 has been processed you should receive a packet from IRS with a copy of IRS Publication 15 (Employer's Tax Guide or "Circular E"), which contains federal withholding tax tables, rules on making your tax deposits, and other essential information. If you don't receive a copy of Publication 15 you can download one at www.irs.gov. Note: You can find additional information on Employer ID numbers at:
https://www.irs.gov/Businesses/Small-Business-&-Self-Employed/Employer-ID-Numbers-EINs

Q: **What's next?**
A: You also need to register your company with the state (or states) where you're doing business. You can find links to various state government web sites at www.irs.gov:
(http://www.irs.gov/Businesses/Small-Businesses-&-Self-Employed/State-Links-1). You will probably need a state identification number and it's usually helpful if you've already received your federal EIN. In any case you will need information about state withholding tax and state unemployment tax requirements.

Q: **What about payroll taxes?**
A: Your payroll tax liability primarily consists of the Social Security, Medicare, federal and state income tax withheld from your employees' wages plus the employer's matching share of Social Security and Medicare taxes (6.2% of Social Security taxable wages and 1.45% of Medicare taxable wages). In addition, employers normally have to pay state and federal unemployment taxes (SUTA and FUTA). The current FUTA rate is 6.0% of your employees' taxable wages but you can take a credit of up to 5.4% for SUTA taxes that you pay (unless the state you operate in is a "credit reduction" state). There is also a $7,000 taxable wage limit on FUTA, which means you stop paying FUTA on an

employee once his or her taxable wages reach $7,000. Generally, your SUTA tax rate is based on the number of unemployment claims filed by employees that you have terminated, but you need to check with your state about the SUTA rate assigned to you and your state's SUTA taxable wage limit (both of which may change from year to year). Some states may also have additional withholding requirements – for example, Alaska, New Jersey, and Pennsylvania require employers to withhold state unemployment insurance from employee wages.

Note: When an employee reaches $200,000 in FICA taxable earnings for the year, the employer has to withhold an additional 0.9% in Medicare tax from that person's wages, making the employees Medicare tax rate 2.35%. The employer's Medicate matching rate stays at 1.45% - the increase applies only to the employee.

Q: **What do I do about depositing payroll taxes?**
A: Social Security, Medicare and income tax amounts that have been withheld from employees' wages normally have to be deposited on either a monthly or semiweekly schedule (which schedule you use for the current calendar year is based on the amount of taxes you reported during the four quarters in your look-back period for 941 filers or the "look-back" year for 944 filers. For details on look-back periods refer to Chapter 11 of Publication 15 - Employer's Tax Guide). Under the monthly schedule taxes on wages paid during a calendar month have to be deposited by the 15th of the following month (or if the 15th is a holiday, by the next business day following the 15th). For semiweekly depositors, taxes on wages paid on Wednesday, Thursday or Friday must be deposited by the following Wednesday. Taxes on wages paid on Saturday, Sunday, Monday or Tuesday must be deposited by the following Friday. If the due date for a semiweekly deposit falls on a holiday you have until the next business day to make your tax deposit. Whether you are a monthly or semiweekly depositor if you have a tax liability of $100,000 or more for a particular pay date you must make your deposit on the next business day - and if you were a monthly depositor, you automatically become a semi-weekly depositor for the remainder of the calendar year and for the following calendar year. Note: If your tax liability is less than $2,500 a quarter you can submit your tax payment with your Form 941 or Form 944 (if filed on time). Refer to IRS Publication 15 (Circular E) and Publication 966 (Electronic Federal Tax Payment System).

Q: **How do I make payroll tax payments?**
A: All federal tax deposits have to be made electronically. Generally, electronic fund transfers are made using the Electronic Federal Tax

Payment System (EFTPS). If you're a new employer you will need to enroll in the EFTPS. The process of enrolling is fairly easy; go to www.eftps.gov and click on the button to open a new account. Enter your EIN (Employer Identification Number), the name of your business and your contact information. Then select your payment option – whether you want to have IRS debit your account directly (the "debit" or standard option) or if you want your financial institution to initiate the transfer (the "credit" option). If you want to use the credit option you will need to check with your financial institution to see if it offers this service (in most cases the debit option is the best choice). The next step is to set any payment limits you want and then enter your bank account information. Once you've completed the setup process you should receive a packet from EFTPS within 15 days that will include your PIN (Personal Identification Number). At that point you can start making payments through EFTPS either by phone or over the internet.

Note: If your payroll taxes for the previous or current quarter are less than $2500 you can remit your taxes with your Form 941 or Form 944 rather than making regular tax deposits as long as your return is filed on time.

Q: **What payroll forms do I need to file and when do I send them?**
A: As an employer, there are a number of federal and state (and possibly city or county) payroll reports that you are required to file. Federal forms include:

- Form 941 (Employer's Quarterly Federal Tax Return) – The 941 is basically a record of the employer's federal tax liability and tax deposits for a given quarter. It includes the gross taxable wages paid for the quarter, the employee and employer Social Security and Medicare tax amounts, and the federal income tax withheld during the quarter. For semiweekly depositors Form 941 must be accompanied by a Schedule B (Report of Tax Liability for Semiweekly Schedule Depositors), which lists the employer's tax liability by day for each day in the quarter. The due date for sending the 941 (and Schedule B) to IRS is the last day of the month following the end of the quarter.
- Form 941-X (Supporting Statement to Correct Information) – Used to correct income and tax information previously reported on Forms 941, 943 and 945.
- Form 944 (Employer's Annual Federal Tax Return) – Form 944 includes the same information as the 941, but for the entire year. Businesses with less than $1,000 in taxes withheld for the year may use Form 944 instead of Form 941 – IRS will notify you if you are required to report payroll taxes annually on

the 944 rather than quarterly with Form 941. Due date for filing the 944 is the end of January of the next year.

ą Form 944-X (Adjusted Employer's Annual Federal Tax Return or Claim for Refund) – Used to correct income and tax information previously reported on Form 944.

ą Form 943 (Employer's Annual Federal Tax Return for Agriculture Employees) – Form 943 is similar to the 941 but for employers who employ farm workers. Form 943 is filed annually for employers who have paid more than $2,500 in wages during the calendar year (for all employees).

ą Form 945 (Annual Return of Withheld Federal Income Tax) – Used to report federal income tax withheld from non-payroll payments (including pensions, gambling winnings, and certain government payments). All federal income tax withholding reported on Forms 1099 or Form W-2G has to be reported on Form 945 (do not use Form 945 to report federal income tax withholding from wages).

ą Form 940 (Employer's Annual Federal Unemployment Tax Return) – Form 940 is a record of the FUTA taxable wages paid to all employees and the federal unemployment tax paid by the employer during the calendar year. Form 940 should be filed by the end of January of the following year.

ą **Form W-2** – (Wage and Tax Statement) is an IRS tax form used to report wages paid to employees and the taxes withheld from them. The W-2 is used by employees to prepare their federal tax returns and to report FICA taxes to the Social Security Administration.

ą **Form W-2c** – (Corrected Wage and Tax Statement) is used to correct errors on W-2 forms previously filed with the Social Security Administration.

ą Form 1099-MISC – You need to fill out a 1099-MISC form at the end of the year to send to any individual (non-employee) or company that you paid $600 or more to during the year in rents, royalties, commissions, fees, prizes and awards (you do not have to send a 1099-MISC to corporations – just individuals, independent contractors, partnerships, LLCs and other non-incorporated organizations). Enter rent payments in Box 1, royalties in Box 2, and other non-employee compensation in Box 7 and enter any federal or state income tax withheld in Box 4 and Box 16. Form 1099-MISC is a multi-part form with copies for the IRS, the payer, the recipient, and state or local tax departments. In addition, a Form 1096 (Annual Summary and Transmittal of U.S. Information Returns) must accompany copies of 1099-MISC forms that you mail to the IRS. 1099 forms can also be trasmitted electronically using the FIRE system (http://fire.irs.gov). Recipients should have their copies by January 31st and the IRS copies are also due by January 31st 2017.

Note: Employers are also required to report any federal tax withheld from non-payroll earnings (such as payments to independent contractors, pension payments, annuities, royalties and gambling winnings) on Form 945 which is filed annually. All federal income tax withholding (referred to as "backup withholding") that is included on Forms 1099 or W2-G must be reported on Form 945 which is due by the end of January for the preceding year (Note: if you made all deposits on time you may file by February 10th). The backup withholding rate is set at 28% of the amount paid. Do not report federal income tax (FIT) withheld on distributions to participants in non-qualified pension plans (such as 457(b) plans) – those amounts should be reported on the 941 or 944. Note: Payments to independent contractors are subject to mandatory "backup withholding" if the contractor has failed to provide a taxpayer identification number to the employer or has provided an incorrect taxpayer identification number.

Q: **What amounts are reported in Box 12 of Form W-2?**
A: Box 12 is used to report the following types of compensation and benefits:

- A – Uncollected Social Security or RRTA (RailRoad Tax Authority) tax on tips
- B – Uncollected Medicare tax on tips (but not Additional Medicare Tax)
- C – Taxable cost of group-term life insurance over $50,000 (included in the wages in boxes 1, 3 and 5)
- D – Elective deferrals to a section 401(k) cash or other deferred compensation plan (including a SIMPLE 401(k) arrangement)
- E – Elective deferrals under a section 403(b) salary reduction agreement
- F – Elective deferrals under a section 408(k)(6) salary reduction SEP
- G – Elective deferrals and employer contributions (including non-elective deferrals) to a section 457(b) deferred compensation plan
- H – Elective deferrals to a section 501(c)(18)(D) tax-exempt organization plan
- J – Nontaxable sick pay
- K – 20% excise tax on excess golden parachute payments
- L – Substantiated employee business expense reimbursements

- M – Uncollected Social Security or RRTA tax on taxable cost of group-term life insurance over $50,000 (former employees only)
- N – Uncollected Medicare tax on taxable cost of group-term life insurance over $50,000 (but not Additional Medicare Tax) (former employees only)
- P – Excludable moving expense reimbursements paid directly to employee
- Q – Nontaxable combat pay
- R – Employer contributions to an Archer MSA
- S – Employee salary reduction contributions under a section 408(p) SIMPLE plan
- T – Adoption benefits
- V – Income from exercise of non-statutory stock option(s)
- W – Employer contributions (including employee contributions through a cafeteria plan) to an employee's health savings account (HSA)
- Y – Deferrals under a section 409A non-qualified deferred compensation plan
- Z – Income under a non-qualified deferred compensation plan that fails to satisfy section 409A
- AA – Designated Roth contributions under a section 401(k) plan
- BB – Designated Roth contributions under a section 403(b) plan
- CC – HIRE exempt wages and tips (2010 only)
- DD – Cost of employer-sponsored health coverage
- EE – Designated Roth contributions under a governmental section 457(b) plan

Q: Can I file my Form 941, Form 944 and/or Form 940 online?
A: Yes, IRS provides an online filing option for Forms 941, 944 and 940. Business filers can apply to IRS for permission to transmit these forms electronically using a provider approved by IRS (that is, a third-party transmitter). Check the IRS website (www.irs.gov) for more information on how to file online and for a list of third-party providers.

Q: Can I file my W-2 forms electronically?
A: If you have 250 or more W-2 forms you must file electronically using the Social Security Administration's Business Services Online (BSO) web service (www.ssa.gov/employer). You also have the option to file electronically regardless of how many W-2s you have. To transmit your information online you must register with the Social Security Administration. Once you've registered with SSA you can log in to the BSO system and send forms W-2 and W-2c (the form used to correct a previously submitted W-2) to SSA by uploading a specially formatted

electronic file (or you can key the information directly into an online form). You can download Social Security Administration Publication No. 42-007 (Specifications for Filing Forms W-2 Electronically [EFW2] from the SSA website (currently http://www.ssa.gov/employer/efw/10efw2.pdf). There are also commercial programs available (such as W2 Mate, Tax Forms Helper, and others that allow you to key in or import W-2 (or 1099) information and create a file that can be transmitted to the SSA.

Note: All W-2, W-2c and W-3 forms are submitted to the Social Security Administration; do not send W-2 information to the IRS. SSA forwards the information to the Internal Revenue Service.

Q: **Can I file my 1099 forms electronically?**
A: If you have 250 or more 1099 returns you must file your returns electronically, but the IRS encourages everyone to submit their 1099 data using its online service called the FIRE (Filing Information Returns Electronically) system (http://fire.irs.gov). Your 1099 information must be in a specially formatted file (see IRS Publication 1220) and you must have a Transmitter Control Code (TCC). To obtain a Transmitter Control Code submit Form 4419 to IRS -- once your application is approved the TCC will be forwarded to you (be sure to submit Form 4419 at least 30 days before the due date of your 1099 returns).

Q: **What type of payroll reports do I need my payroll system to produce each pay period?**
A: Your payroll should provide the following types of reports:
- Payroll Register – Lists all employees who were paid, showing their gross pay, taxes withheld, voluntary or other deductions and net pay. If an employee is contributing to a retirement fund and the employer provides a matching contribution, the employer match amount should also be shown. In addition the payroll register often includes month-to-date and year-to-date amounts for each employee along with totals by department and overall totals for all employees.
- Payroll Tax Register – Shows all taxes withheld along with employer matching amounts for Social Security and Medicare taxes and the employer's total federal tax deposit for the period.
- Checks and/or Deposit Slips – Employees who are paid by check should receive a pay check which includes a stub showing gross earnings, deductions and net pay. Employees who are paid through direct deposit should receive a "deposit advice" of some type which shows the same information as on a payroll check stub.
- Payroll Ledger – A payroll ledger of some type should be kept

for each employee and updated each payroll. The ledger should show each employee's accumulated earnings, taxes, deductions and net pay.

ą   Additional reports may include a voluntary deduction register, department summary report, 401(k) listing, cafeteria plan report, and a bank reconciliation report.

Q: **What reports or forms do I need to produce at year-end?**
A: Each employee should receive a Form W-2 (Wage and Tax Statement) by the end of January for the previous year, showing taxable wages and income tax, Social Security, and Medicare taxes withheld for the year. In addition if you paid an individual (non-employee) or company $600 or more for services rendered during the year, you need to send that person or company a 1099-MISC form showing the total amount paid and any taxes withheld (Note: you do not need to send a 1099-MISC to corporations). You will also need to submit your W-2 information to the Social Security Administration and any 1099 data to the IRS. Currently you may also need to produce 1095-C forms for all full-time employees (and copies for the IRS) if you employ 50 or more full-time (and full-time equivalent) employees.

Q: **Do I have to have Workers' Compensation Insurance?**
A: All businesses with employees are required to carry Workers' Compensation Insurance coverage either through a commercial carrier, on a self-insured basis, or through your state's Workers' Compensation Insurance program. For further information on your state's insurance program check on the state agency links at:
www.nolo.com/legal-encyclopedia/workers-compensation-basics-employers-30333.html

Q: **What are Workers' Compensation insurance premiums based on?**
A: The premiums are based on your business classification, your employees occupational classification codes and the total net amount of overtime premiums paid.

Q: **Are Workers' Compensation benefits taxable?**
A: No. Workers' Compensation benefits are not federal or state taxable and are not included on the W-2.

Q: **Is all Workers' Compensation insurance handled through state administered funds?**
A: No. Arizona, California, Colorado, Idaho, Maryland, Michigan, Montana, New York, Oklahoma, Oregon, Pennsylvania and Utah allow

employers to choose between the state administered fund and private insurers.

Q: **How do I record payroll information in the general ledger?**
A: Entries to the general ledger from payroll can become fairly complex, especially if you are allocating wages, taxes and other deductions between different cost centers in your company. The most basic case though would involve two entries. The first journal entry would debit a salaries and wages account for the total earnings paid and credit the appropriate accounts for deductions such as Social Security tax payable, Medicare tax payable, federal income tax payable, state income tax payable, United Way, Uniforms, and so on. This first entry would also include a credit to an account such as Cash in Bank or Accrued Payroll for the net amount of the payroll. A second journal entry would debit an account like "Payroll Tax Expense" and credit the appropriate accounts for the employer matching share of Social Security and Medicare taxes and the employer's state and federal unemployment taxes. When the withheld taxes or other payables (such as 401(k) amounts) are remitted another journal entry would be made debiting the taxes or other amounts payable and crediting an account such as "cash in bank".

Employees

Q: **Should I have an employee job application form?**
A: Every business should have an application form of some type. It can provide a complete record as to an applicant's background including: name, address, phone number, social security number, educational background, previous employment and experience, references and special skills or qualifications.

Q: **What payroll information do I need from my employees?**
A: You need to have each of your employees fill out a Form W-4 (Employee's Withholding Allowance Certificate) so you can withhold the correct federal income tax. By filling out Form W-4 the employee indicates his or her marital status, the number of withholding exemptions claimed, any additional withholding amount desired, and (in some cases) a credit claimed for child care expenses and/or a child tax credit. An employee can also claim an exemption from withholding for the current year if he or she had tax withheld in the previous year but had no tax liability and expects to have no tax liability in the current year. IRS can request a copy of any employee's W-4 but unless you receive such a request just keep a current W-4 in your files for each employee. In addition, every new employee has to fill out a Form I-9 before starting work and produce documents verifying his or her identity and work eligibility (such as a valid driver's license, social security card, voter registration card or birth certificate).

Q: **What is E-Verify?**
A: E-Verify is an Internet-based system run by the Department of Homeland Security that allows employers to determine the eligibility of employees to work in the United States. E-Verify matches information from the person's Employment Eligibility Verification Form I-9 against U.S. Government records – if the information matches the person is eligible to work in the United States. If you have an employee who has applied for a Social Security number but hasn't received it, he or she may work while waiting for a number to be issued. The employer should complete a Form I-9, but wait to use E-Verify until the employee receives his or her SSN. You can access the E-Verify system at:
   http://www.dhs.gov/e-verify
Note: You must enroll in E-Verify in order to use this service.

Q; **What is "New Hire reporting"?**
A: The Personal Responsibility and Work Opportunity Reconciliation Act of 1996 requires all employers to report newly hired or re-hired

19

employees to the appropriate state agency within 20 days of the person's hire date (you can find links to state agencies that handle new hire reporting and information as to reporting requirements for each state at http://www.sba.gov/content/new-hire-reporting-your-state).

Q: **Who is an Employee?**
A: Anyone who performs services for you is your employee if you can control both what will be done and how it will be done.

Q: **Who is an Independent Contractor?**
A: Basically, anyone who does work for you but isn't an employee. Employers can tell an independent contractor what to do and when the work should be completed, but not how to go about doing the job or what hours the contractor has to work.

Q: **What are "Statutory employees"?**
A: Statutory employees are somewhere between independent contractors and regular employees. They are workers in certain occupations who wouldn't normally be considered employees, but who have been declared employees under the federal tax laws so that their employer normally has to withhold FICA taxes (Social Security and Medicare tax) from their wages. Employers should not withhold federal income tax from statutory employees unless the employee is subject to backup withholding. Workers that may qualify as statutory employees include: full-time life insurance agents working primarily for a single company, as well as certain types of salespeople, home workers and truck drivers. Statutory employees receive a W-2 form at the end of the year just like any other employee. You can find more information on statutory employees at:
https://www.irs.gov/Businesses/Small-Businesses-&-Self-Employed/Statutory-Employees

Q: **Who are "statutory non-employees"?**
A: Direct sellers, certain companion sitters and qualified real estate agents are considered non-employees and are usually treated as self-employed for federal tax purposes, so no federal income tax, Social Security tax, Medicare tax or FUTA tax is withheld or reported.

Q: **What constitutes an "Independent contractor"?**
A: The general rule for defining someone doing work for you as an independent contractor (as opposed to a regular employee) is that you, the employer, have the right to control only the result of the work done by that person, not the means or method of accomplishing the work. If you can't decide whether a person or persons working for you should be

classified as an employee or independent contractor, you can file Form SS-8, Determination of Worker Status for Purposes of Federal Employment Taxes and Income Tax Withholding with the IRS. They will review the information on the form and determine the worker's status. The drawback is that it can take at least six months to get a decision, but if you have a number of people whose status is in question it may be a good idea to go ahead and file an SS-8. Misclassification of an employee as an independent contractor can result in major penalties: federal tax assessed at 1.5% of the wages paid to the individual, 100% of the employer share of Social Security and Medicare taxes, plus 20% of the employee share of Social Security and Medicare taxes. Note: Certain workers are automatically considered employees: officers of corporations who provide services to the corporation, food and laundry drivers, full-time salespeople who sell goods for resale, full-time life insurance agents working mainly for one company, and at-home workers who are supplied with material and given specifications for work to be performed.

Q: **Who is a "Common-Law employee"?**
A: Under common-law rules, anybody who performs services for you is your employee if you control both what will be done and how it will be done. Even if you let the employee accomplish the work in his own way, as long as you have the right to control the way the work is done that person is an employee and not an independent contractor.

Q: **What is the "Common Law Test"?**
A: The IRS uses a 20 question test to assess how much control an employer has over a worker in order to determine if that person is an employee or an independent contractor ("Yes" answers tend to indicate an employer-employee relationship):
1) Is the worker required to follow the employer's instructions in completing the job or accomplishing a task?
2) Does the employer provide the training necessary for completion of the job?
3) Are the worker's specific personal services required for successful completion of the job?
4) Are the worker's services crucial to the success or continued existence of the company?
5) Does the employer set work hours?
6) Does the worker have a continuing relationship with the company?
7) Does the employer hire, supervise or pay any of the worker's assistants?
8) Is the worker precluded from seeking assignments with other

companies or from refusing assignments offered by the employer?

9) Does the employer specify the location where the work must be performed?
10) Does the employer direct the order or sequence of tasks to be performed?
11) Does the employer require regular progress reports?
12) Is the worker paid by the hour, week or month, rather than for completion (or stage of completion) of the project?
13) Does the worker work only for the employer?
14) Does the employer pay business overhead and incidental expenses?
15) Does the employer provide equipment, tools and materials?
16) Is the work performed on the employer's premises or using the employer's facilities?
17) Are the worker's services not available to the general public?
18) Does the employer provide a minimum "salary" and therefore shield the worker from the risk of profit or loss on the job.
19) Does the employer have the right to terminate the worker even if the job results are achieved?
20) Is the employer required to pay the worker for time spent even if the job is not completed?

Q: **What is IRS Section 530?**

A: Section 530 specifies certain cases where an employee may be considered an independent contractor. Under Section 530, an individual will not be considered an employee if the employer treated him or her (and other workers performing similar tasks) as non-employees for all periods, had a reasonable basis for doing so, and filed the required information and other returns (such as Form 1099-MISC) on a consistent basis. Employees specifically excluded from 530 protection include technical service specialists such as engineers and computer programmers.

Q: **Are sole proprietors and partners in a partnership employees?**

A: Sole proprietors and partners in a business are neither employees or independent contractors – they pay their own income tax and Social Security/Medicare self-employment tax. However shareholders in an incorporated business are legally an employee of the corporation in most cases (Officers/Shareholders in a corporation who don't perform any serivces – or only minor services – and are not entitled to compensation are not considered employees).

Q: **What's the difference between "exempt employees" and "non-**

exempt employees"?

A: Under the FLSA (Fair Labor Standards Act) employees have to be paid at least the minimum hourly wage and must be paid overtime for hours worked over 40 hours a week. However the law provides for an exemption from these rules for employees working in an executive, administrative or professional capacity, outside salespeople, and certain employees in computer related positions. To be classified as "exempt" an employee has to fit into one of the classes listed above and has to be paid on a salary basis (meaning the employee has to receive the full salary each week regardless of the number of hours worked). Also, to qualify for the exemption an employee must be paid at least $455 per week. For further information check the Department of Labor web site at http://www.dol.gov.

Q: What are the laws governing hiring of teenagers?

A: There are both federal and state "child labor" laws. There are only a few jobs that youngsters under the age of 14 can be hired to do (such as newspaper carrier). For teenagers 14 or over but under age 18 there are certain occupations that are prohibited (such as meat cutter, jobs requiring the use of heavy machinery, hazardous material handling, etc.) and there are usually restrictions on working hours. In every case, an employer should make sure to have some proof of age for workers under 18 and the permission of a parent or guardian. Because of the number and complexity of many state child labor laws, you should also check with the Department of Labor in your particular state before hiring teenage employees.

Q: What do I do in the case of an employee's death?

A: If you're ever faced with the death of an employee, any unpaid wages (salary, vacation pay, sick leave, etc.) should be paid to the employee's beneficiary or to his or her estate. You will also need to send a Form 1099-Misc to the estate or beneficiary and report that final payment in box 3 ("Other income"). In addition, if the accrued wages are paid in the same year as the employee's death, the employer must withhold FICA (Social Security and Medicare) tax from those wages and include them on the deceased employee's W-2 as FICA taxable earnings. However, if the payment is made in a year following the employee's death, then no FICA withholding is required and the earnings do not have to be reported as FICA taxable. In either case the wages paid to a deceased employee are exempt from federal income tax withholding (and they are usually exempt from state withholding as well). Note: If the wages are paid in the same year as the employee's death they are normally subject to both FUTA and SUTA tax.

In the case where a paycheck has already been issued to the employee but the employee dies before cashing it, the check has to be reissued for the net amount, payable to the employee's beneficiary or a personal representative. The employer should make sure that the person receiving the check signs a statement that the money is being paid for a deceased employee's uncashed paycheck. The necessary taxes have already been withheld (on the original paycheck) so the wages and taxes will automatically be included in the employee's W-2 at the end of the year.

Example: John Doe, who worked for ABC Company passed away on August 14th. The company owed him a total of $1,980 in accumulated pay and vacation pay. A check was issued to his wife the next week for $1,828.53 ($1,980 less $122.76 in Social Security tax and $28.71 in Medicare tax) and a 1099-MISC form was also issued to his wife at the end of the year with $1,980 reported in Box 3 (Other Income) along with John's W-2.

Q: Is there a way to verify an employee's social security number?
A: Yes, you can go to http://www.ssa.gov/employer/ssnv.htm and check for valid social security numbers. You do have to register however in order to make use of Business Services Online.

Foreign Employees

Q: Do I need to withhold any taxes on foreign employees working in their home country?

A: If you have residents of a foreign country performing services for you in their own country, there is no U.S. withholding. There are no documents specifically required where payments are to foreigners outside this country -- however, it's a good idea to carefully document everything in situations like this in case IRS has questions at some point.

Q: What about foreign employees working in this country?
A: IRS has two separate tax systems: the resident alien tax system and the nonresident alien tax system. Resident aliens pay taxes on their worldwide income just the same as any U.S. citizen; non-resident aliens pay taxes only on their U.S.-source income. All foreign employees must complete Form UC W-8BEN (Certificate of Foreign Status for Federal Tax Withholding) -- this form is used to determine whether someone is a resident or nonresident alien for tax purposes. Resident aliens are subject to Social Security and Medicare tax and so are non-resident aliens (unless they hold an F-1 or J-1 visa). As for federal and state income tax withholding, aliens are subject to the same state withholding laws as U.S. citizens. Federal withholding is more complicated -- for example non-resident aliens from countries which have a tax treaty agreement with the United States may be able to exempt part or all of their income from federal withholding.

Q: Are foreign employees eligible for unemployment benefits?
A: In general, foreign employees are not eligible for unemployment benefits (or for Medicare coverage).

Wages / Taxable Wages

Q: **What are gross wages?**
A: Gross pay is total wages before any deductions (taxes or other deductions). If you pay an employee 12 dollars per hour for 40 hours of work, the employee's gross pay is $480.

Q: **What types of compensation are considered taxable wages?**
A: Taxable wages include most types of compensation, such as wages and salaries, tips, vacation allowances, bonuses, commissions, cash awards, and gift certificates. Meals and lodging furnished for the employee's convenience are also considered to be taxable. You can refer to IRS Publication 525 (Taxable and Nontaxable Income) for more detailed information on what IRS classifies as taxable compensation. Also, IRS Publication 15-A contains additional information on wages and Publication 15-B provides information on many other forms of compensation including:
- Accident and health benefits
- Health Savings Accounts
- Group term life insurance coverage
- Lodging and meals
- De minimus (minimal) benefits
- Dependent care assistance
- Educational assistance
- Employee discounts
- Employee stock options

Q: **How do I calculate an employee's wages?**
A: Salaried employees are normally paid a fixed amount each pay period (usually their annual salary divided by the number of pay periods per year). To figure an hourly employee's pay, you multiply the individual's hourly rate of pay times the number of hours worked in the pay period. If an employee worked over 40 hours in a given one week period, you would pay him for 40 hours times his normal rate of pay plus the number of hours over 40 times his rate of pay times an overtime factor (usually 1.5). Employees may also be paid on a piece rate or on a commission basis.

Q: **Do I have to keep track of salaried employees' time?**
A: It's a good idea to keep a record of some type but it's up to the employer to decide whether to require salaried employees to track their hours worked.

Q: **How do I keep track of hourly employees' time?**
A: It can be as simple as having them fill out a time sheet each day or as sophisticated as a biometric time clock system or a web-based time accounting system. The important thing is to have as accurate a system as possible with as little hassle for your employees as possible.

Q: **What do I need to know about the minimum wage?**

A: The Fair Labor Standards Act contains mandatory standards for federal minimum wage rates. Non-exempt employees paid on an hourly basis must receive at least the federal minimum wage for each hour worked. For employees paid on some basis other than hourly (piece-rate, commission, etc.), their pay must be at least equivalent to the number of hours worked times the federal minimum wage. Many states also have minimum wage laws; in those states that do, the employee is entitled to whichever rate is higher - federal or state minimum wage rate. Every employer with employees subject to the Fair Labor Standards Act is required to post a notice explaining the Act in a conspicuous place so workers can read it. Note: The federal minimum wage for non-exempt employees was raised in May of 2007 increasing it from $5.15 per hour to:

$5.85 per hour, effective July 24th 2007
$6.55 per hour, effective July 24th 2008
$7.25 per hour, effective July 24th 2009

NOTE: States with minimum wage levels greater than federal minimum (as of 2017):

- Alaska - $8.75 per hour
- Arkansas - $8.50
- Arizona - $8.05 per hour
- California - $10.00 per hour ($10.55 if more than 25 employees) (some counties have higher minimum wage amounts)
- Colorado - $8.31 per hour
- Connecticut - $9.60 per hour
- Delaware - $8.25 per hour
- District of Columbia - $11.50 per hour
- Florida - $8.10 per hour
- Hawaii - $9.25 per hour ($10.10 in 2018)
- Illinois - $8.25 per hour
- Maine - $7.50 per hour
- Maryland - $8.75 per hour
- Massachusetts - $11.00 per hour

- Michigan - $8.50 per hour
- Maryland - $8.75 per hour ($9.25 on 7-01-2017)
- Minnesota – $7.75 per hour (for employers with $500,000 or more in sales per year: $9.50 per hour)
- Missouri - $7.65 per hour (Kansas City: $9.00/hr, St. Louis: $10.00/hr)
- Montana - $8.15 per hour
- Nebraska - $9.00 per hour
- Nevada - $8.25 per hour with no health benefits provided by employer - $7.25 with health benefits provided by employer
- New Jersey - $8.44 per hour
- New York - $9.70 per hour (New York City: $13.13/hr without health insurance, $11.50/hr with health insurance)
- New Mexico - $7.50 per hour
- Ohio - $8.15 per hour ($7.25/hr if gross sales less than $299,000)
- Oregon - $9.25 per hour
- Rhode Island - $9.60 per hour
- South Dakota - $8.65 per hour
- Vermont - $10.00 per hour
- Washington - $9.53 per hour
- West Virginia - $8.75 per hour

Q: **Is there a different minimum wage for young people?**
A: Workers under 20 years old can be paid at a rate below the federal minimum wage for the first 90 days of employment (but not less than $4.25 per hour).

Q: **If a salaried employee only works part of a day can I pay him just part of his daily salary?**
A: No, if a salaried employee works any part of a work day you have to pay him or her for a full day's work. However, if a salaried employee doesn't perform any work in a given week you don't have to pay him or her for that week.

Q: **Do I have to pay a salaried employee for vacation or sick days?**
A: Salaried employees are often entitled to a certain number of vacation and sick days each year. If one of your salaried people calls in sick or takes vacation days, he is paid for the full day or days if he has the hours available; if he doesn't have any hours left you do not have to pay him for that time.

Q: **Do I have to pay hourly employees for time off on holidays?**

A: No, you are not required to pay hourly employees for time off on a holiday.

Q: **Do I have to count paid time off as hours worked in determining overtime pay?**
A: No. An employee has to actually work over 40 hours in a week to qualify for overtime pay. Paid time off (vacation, sick leave, holidays, etc.) is not considered time worked (unless there is a collective bargaining agreement in place that states otherwise).

Q: **If an employee takes work home and does it there after normal working hours do I have to pay the employee for that time?**
A: In general, yes you do. Any time spent by an employee doing productive work for the employer is considered as "hours worked" under FLSA rules.

Q: **If employees are allowed to take two coffee breaks during the day does that time automatically count as hours worked?**
A: If a rest period or coffee break lasts 20 minutes or less that time should be counted as hours worked.

Q: **How can I calculate an hourly rate for a salaried employee?**
A: Divide the employee's annual salary by 2080 (52 weeks times 40 hours per week, the standard number of work hours per year).

Q: **Do I have to pay minimum wage to my employees who receive tips?**
A: Not necessarily. An employer can pay less than the federal minimum wage (or state minimum wage if higher than federal) if the employee's tip income plus his or her direct wages at least equal the minimum wage hourly rate times the hours worked.

Q: **Do I have to pay minimum wage to full-time students?**
A: Retail or service businesses and farms can hire full-time students (who are of working age) and pay them at 85% of minimum wage (subject to state laws).

Q: **My teenage son works for me – do I have to withhold taxes from his paycheck?**
A: If you have a son or daughter under 18 working for you, his or her wages are not subject to Social Security and Medicare taxes as long as your business is a sole proprietorship or a partnership where each partner is one of the child's parents. Also, the child's earnings are not subject to federal unemployment tax until he or she turns 21. However,

payments for the services of a child of any age who works in a parent's business are usually subject to income tax withholding.

Q: My husband is one of my employees – is his pay subject to withholding?
A: A person employed by his or her spouse in a sole proprietorship is subject to income tax withholding and Social Security and Medicare taxes, but not FUTA (federal unemployment) tax.

Q: Do I need to take out withholding tax on an employee advance?
A: No, just pay the employee the flat amount of the advance – but be sure to deduct that same amount from his or her next paycheck.

Q: What are "supplemental wages"?
A: Payments such as commissions or bonuses are considered by the IRS to be "supplemental" wages -- that is, money separate from an employee's regular income such as bonuses, commissions, severance pay, sick pay, retroactive pay increases and so forth. If you pay supplemental wages separately from an employee's regular wages the IRS requires that you withhold a flat 25% for federal withholding tax or use a formula to determine the withholding tax (see IRS Publication 15 for details). If you combine the supplemental and regular wages as a lump sum, then you withhold tax as if the total amount was a single payment for a regular pay period (note that this generally results in regular wages being more highly taxed than normal). For more information on types of supplemental pay and how to handle it, look at the appropriate section of your Circular E (IRS Pub 15).

Q: Are gifts to employees considered as part of their wages?
A: Yes, cash or cash equivalents such as watches, trips to Las Vegas, or a few shares of company stock are almost always considered taxable income, regardless of the amount. The only exception might be something like a company-wide drawing for a certain item, where the item is of relatively small value (in other words, not something like a new car).

Q: Are employee dependent care benefits considered wages?
A: Dependent care services you directly or indirectly pay for (or provide to an employee under a dependent care assistance program) to allow the employee to work may qualify as an excludable benefit. Generally, dependent care assistance up to a certain amount (currently $5,000 for married couples or $2500 for married employees filing separate returns) is not taxable. At year end the total amount of dependent care benefits provided to an employee should be reported in box 10 of the employee's

Form W-2 and any excess amount over the $5,000 or $2500 limit should be included in box 1, 3 and 5. For more information see IRS Publication 503 (Qualifying Person Test and Work-Related Expense Test).

Q: **What is a "tipped" employee?**
A: According to the Department of Labor, a tipped employee is one who "customarily and regularly" receives more than $30 in tips each month.

Q: **How do I handle tips?**
A: Tips are defined as payments made by customers of their own free will and in whatever amount they wish. If a restaurant includes a mandatory "gratuity" with each check, that gratuity is not considered a "tip" and is simply treated as normal taxable wages when it's distributed to the employee. Cash tips however, if voluntarily given, are not taxable wages for an employee if they run less than $20 in a month and are reported to the employer by the 10th of the following month (using Form 4070 and Form 4070A). Once the $20 limit is exceeded though, all cash tips for that employee (including the initial $20) become taxable income and should be reported to the employer on whatever form the employer provides (which can be paper or electronic) or on Form 4070 (Employee's Report of Tips to Employer) and Form 4070A (Employee's Daily Record of Tips). The employer is required to collect Social Security, Medicare and income tax withholding on taxable tips the same as on regular wages, and to pay the employer's share of the Social Security and Medicare taxes on the tips, along with with the appropriate FUTA tax.

Q: **What is the minimum pay rate for a tipped employee?**
A: You are only required to pay $2.13 an hour to tipped employees (employees who earn at least $30 a month in tips) if that amount plus the person's tip income at least equals the federal minimum wage (or state minimum wage if greater than federal). The difference between $2.13 an hour (or whatever hourly wage the tipped employee is paid) and the federal minimum wage hourly rate is generally referred to as a "tip credit".

Q: **What if the taxes on an employee's tips are more than that person's wages?**
A: Your obligation to withhold the employee's FICA and income taxes is limited to what can be withheld from the person's non-tip wages. If the non-tip wages aren't sufficient to cover all taxes, withhold taxes in the following order: 1) Withholding taxes on regular wages, 2) Social Security and Medicare taxes on tips, 3) income tax on tips. If you still don't have enough money to cover the employee's FICA taxes, your responsibility to

withhold the uncollected portion ends at that point (income tax shortages should be added to the income tax withholding on the next payroll though).

Q: **What if an employee doesn't report tips given directly to him or her?**
A: If the IRS determines that an employee has failed to report cash tips of over $20 a month to you, you can be held liable for the employer's share of FICA (Social Security and Medicare taxes) and the employee may be penalized the other 50 percent of the FICA tax due on the tips.

Q: **What are allocated tips?**
A: In general, food or beverage establishments that have ten or more tipped employees at work on a typical business day must allocate tip income to employees if the total amount of tips reported by all employees is less than a certain minimum percent (usually eight percent) of total sales. The amount of allocated tips is the difference between the minimum percent of total sales and the actual total of tips reported. The employer does not have to withhold any Social Security, Medicare or income tax on allocated tips, but he must file Form 8027 (Employer's Annual Information Return of Tips Income and Allocated Tips) each year and he must show the amount of allocated tips in box 8 (but not Box 1) of the W-2 for each employee who received allocated tips. Allocated tips can be split or "allocated" among tipped employees on the basis of hours worked, on the basis of each employee's actual gross receipts, or according to a "good faith" agreement between the restaurant and at least two thirds of its tipped employees. Once again, for further information refer to IRS Publication 15 (Circular E), the Employer's Tax Guide.

Q: **Are gratuities and auto-gratuities the same thing as tips?**
A: Although the word gratuity is often used as a synonym for tip, they are not really the same thing. Tips are discretionary amounts decided by the customer. Gratuities are fixed amounts (usually set by the employer) that the customer pays as part of his or her bill and a portion of which may or may not be given to the employees. The IRS has specified that in the case of actual gratuities, those amounts are to be treated as income to the employer and if some portion of the gratuities is distributed to employees, the gratuity amounts are to be included on the employees' paychecks as wages. In addition, since gratuities aren't the same as tips employers can't take a "tip credit" on those amounts even if the gratuities are distributed to the employees. Common examples of auto-gratuities include:
  • Per person cover charges at clubs and restaurants

- Room service surcharges at hotels
- Large party surcharges at restaurants

Q: **What is a "fringe benefit"?**
A: A fringe benefit is a form of pay (including services, property, cash or cash equivalent) in addition to normal pay. Fringe benefits include items such as meals, lodging and reimbursement of moving expenses. Non-monetary fringe benefits that are taxable are valued at their FMV (Fair Market Value); that is, the amount a buyer would be willing to pay for that item or service.

Q: **What fringe benefits are excludable from taxable wages?**
A: There are numerous items that may fall into this category such as employee educational assistance, moving expense reimbursements, and health savings plans. Rather than go over all of them individually you should send for (or download from www.irs.gov) a copy of IRS Publication 15-B, which covers each of these situations in detail.

Q: **Are health benefits excludable from an employee's taxable wages?**
A: Accident and health benefits are normally exempt from income tax withholding (except for long term benefits) and from Social Security and Medicare (except for S corporation employees who are at least 2% shareholders). These types of benefits are also exempt from federal unemployment taxes.

Q: **Is employee group term life insurance coverage taxable?**
A: Employee group term life insurance is exempt from federal income tax withholding and from federal unemployment taxes. It is also exempt from Social Security and Medicare withholding up to $50,000 of coverage - for coverage over $50,000 you have to calculate the cost of the additional coverage (see IRS Publication 15-B for details) and report that amount on the W-2 as wages in boxes 1, 3 and 5, and in box 12 with code "C". To calculate the taxable value of the amount of life insurance over $50,000:
1) Round the amount of life insurance to the nearest $100.
2) Subtract $50,000 from the total amount of coverage.
3) Multiply the number of thousands of dollars of insurance coverage remaining by the cost shown in the table below (accurate for 2016).
4) Calculate the insurance cost for each month during the year.
5) Multiply the monthly amount by 12 to get the annual cost.
6) Subtract any amounts paid by the employee.
7) Include the total amount on the employee's W-2 form.

Table:

Employee Age	Insurance Cost
Under 25	$0.05
25 through 29	$0.06
30 through 34	$0.08
35 through 39	$0.09
40 through 44	$0.10
45 through 49	$0.15
50 through 54	$0.23
55 through 59	$0.43
60 through 64	$0.66
65 through 69	$1.27
70 and over	$2.06

Q: Does the actual cost of group term life insurance coverage matter when determining if the under $50,000 tax exclusion applies?

A: No, the amount of the death benefit determines whether the $50,000 exclusion applies. If the total value of the death benefit for all employer-provided life insurance during a specific period of coverage (usually one month) exceeds $50,000 then the excess is taxable.

Q: Are meals that are provided for employees taxable?

A: No, if the meals are furnished on your business premises for your convenience then they are not taxable.

Q: Is dependent care assistance taxable?

A: Dependent care assistance is exempt from federal taxes up to certain limits. The services must be for a qualifying person's care and must be provided in order to allow the employee to work. Under those conditions, an employee can generally exclude up to $5,000 of benefits from gross income ($2,500 for married employees filing separate returns).

Q: What's involved in providing educational assistance to an employee?

A: Section 127 of the Internal Revenue Code allows employers to provide up to $5,250 per year of educational assistance (tuition, fees, books, supplies, etc.) to an employee, with that money being excluded from the employee's taxable income. Section 127 also applies to employer-provided job and non-job related courses of instruction. Employers who provide educational assistance to their employees can deduct those costs as a business expense if the employer has a written qualified assistance program that is offered on a nondiscriminatory basis and meets all IRS requirements (see Section 127 of the IRC for details).

Q: **Are employee expense reimbursements subject to income tax withholding?**
A: Not if the reimbursement amounts are paid under an accountable plan. An "accountable" plan requires that the employee's expenses be business related, that they be accounted for within a reasonable time period (generally 60 days), and that the employee returns any money over and above the amounts on the expense report that are approved by the company.

Q: **Are employer reimbursed moving expenses taxable to the employee and deductible for the employer?**
A: Employers who pay moving expenses for an employee can pay for whatever expenses they choose to, but only those expenses that qualify as deductible can be excluded from the employee's income. All other expenses paid for by the employer are subject to withholding for federal income, social security, and medicare taxes. The employer is also responsible for FUTA taxes on those payments and, in most states, for state withholding tax. Moving expenses incurred within one year of when the employee started working for the company may be qualified expenses; however the move must have been required by the new job and the expenses must meet two other tests:

- Distance test – The new place of work must be at least 50 miles further from the employee's old residence than his old place of work was from his old residence (i.e. if his old place of work was 15 miles from his old home, his new place of work must be at least 65 miles (15 + 50) from his old residence.
- Time test – The employee must work full-time for at least 39 weeks during the first 12 months after arriving in the general location of his new job. However, the 39 weeks doesn't have to be all with your company and does not have to be all in a row.

The following expenses qualify as deductible moving expenses if the employee meets the tests above:

- Moving the employee's household goods and personal effects.
- Travel expenses for the employee and his/her family from the employee's old home to his or her new home, The expenses can include lodging but not meals. (Note: house-hunting trips do not qualify as deductible expenses).

For further information refer to IRS Publication 521.

Overtime

Q: **What is overtime?**
A: Overtime is simply the amount of time someone works over and beyond normal working hours. So what does that mean to an employer? In the U.S. the Fair Labor Standards Act of 1938 applies to all employees involved in or producing goods for interstate commerce. The FLSA dictates a standard work week of 40 hours for certain types of workers and calls for payment of hours over 40 at a rate of at least 1 and 1/2 times the worker's normal pay rate. FLSA rules do not mandate overtime pay for night work or work on weekends and holidays (although the 40 hours per week rule still applies). In addition, some types of workers (such as independent contractors, agricultural employees, outside salesmen, executives, truck drivers, railroad workers, administrative and professional people) are "exempt" from FLSA standards. Currently, somewhere around 40% of U.S. employees are considered "exempt".

Q: **Who is eligible for overtime pay?**
A: Under the current FLSA overtime rules, employers are required to pay overtime to workers earning less than $23,660 per year ($455 per week) unless they fall under an "exempt" category as noted above. A new Department of Labor regulation raising the overtime eligibility level to $913 per week or $47,476 per year was scheduled to go into effect on December 1, 2016 but that regulation is currently being blocked by a court order. There is a possibility that the regulation may be altered to lower that pay level (or even rescinded).

Q: **What about hospital employees?**
A: Hospitals and their employees may agree to calculate overtime based on a 14-day period rather than a standard workweek.

Q: **What about employees who work on commission?**
A: Employees in retail or service industries who work primarily on commission are exempt from overtime regulations as long as their weekly pay rate including commissions is at least one and a half times minimum wage and more than half their monthly pay comes from commissions.

Q: **If an employee takes work home does that count as hours worked on the job?**
A: In general the answer is "yes". Non-exempt employees (employees governed by the Fair Labor Standards Act or FLSA) have to be paid for

all hours worked, even those outside the regular workplace, and that time counts toward the 40 hours per week used in determining overtime pay.

Q: If I pay an employee for sick time do those hours count in figuring overtime?
A: No, even if an employee is paid for sick time or other absences, those hours do not count toward the 40 hours a week for overtime pay purposes.

Q: What if an employee works at different rates for different jobs during the week?
A: Employers have three options for calculating overtime pay for an employee who worked at different rates during the week:
- Pay for all overtime hours at the higher rate
- Calculate the overtime by taking the employee's total earnings, divide by total hours worked, then take half of this average rate and multiply it by the overtime hours
- Use an overtime rate agreed on in advance with the employee

Q: How do I calculate overtime pay for employees who get paid by the piece?
A: If you have employees who are paid by the number of pieces produced, you have two options for calculating overtime pay. You can pay them, in addition to their piecework earnings, an amount equal to one-half of their hourly rate (calculated as their piecework earnings divided by the number of hours worked that week) multiplied by the number of hours in excess of 40 worked during the week. Alternatively you can (with the agreement of your employees) pay piece-work employees one and one-half times the piece rate for each piece produced during the overtime hours.

Q: Do I have to pay overtime to an employee who works more than 8 hours in a day?
A: Unless there is a state law or a collective bargaining agreement that requires you to pay overtime if someone works more than eight hours in a day, you only have to pay overtime if the employee works more than forty hours during the week.

Q: How do I calculate overtime pay on commissions?
A: Commissions are considered straight-time pay so you divide the amount of the commission by the total number of hours the employee worked during the week the commission was paid in order to get an hourly rate – then the overtime pay is calculated as one-half times that hourly rate times the number of hours worked over 40.

Q: **What else do I need to know about overtime?**

A: The FLSA rules apply to a "workweek" -- an employee's workweek is a fixed (and recurring) period of 168 hours – seven consecutive 24 hour periods. It doesn't have to correspond to a calendar week. It can begin on any day and at any hour. Hours cannot be averaged over two or more workweeks -- the 40 hour rule applies to each week individually. In determining the overtime rate for an employee, the employee's weekly earnings may be calculated on a piece-work, commission or other basis, but overtime pay must be based on the average pay rate for that week. Incidentally, a lump sum paid for work done during overtime hours without regard for the number of hours worked does not qualify as overtime pay (even if the amount exceeds the total of overtime hours times 1 1/2 times the employee's pay rate).

Q: **Do I pay workers' compensation premiums on overtime pay?**

A: In most states you pay workers' compensation premiums only on the "straight time" portion of overtime pay. In other words, your workers' compensation rate is calculated as if all hours are being paid at the employee's normal pay rate, not the time and a half (or double time, etc.) rate that the person receives for overtime.

Q: **Can overtime pay be paid in advance?**

A: Yes. If an employee works less than 40 hours in a week the employer can advance the employee the difference in pay between what he actually made and what he would have been paid if he had worked 40 hours. Then when the employee works over 40 hours in a week this "advance overtime pay" can be offset against the amount of overtime pay owed.

Sick Pay and Disability Insurance

Q: **What do I need to know about sick pay?**
A: Sick pay is income paid to an employee who is absent from work because of illness -- it can come from the employer, from a disability fund, from a welfare fund, or from an insurance company. If sick pay is paid directly by the employer it is generally treated as ordinary taxable wages (although if an employee is absent for an extended period of time, Social Security and Medicare withholding only apply for the first six months). If sick pay is provided by a third party such as an insurance company, income tax withholding doesn't apply unless the employee requests it; however, the insurance company is considered as the employer for FICA tax purposes and is responsible for withholding, depositing and reporting the employee's Social Security and Medicare taxes. However if the third party withholds and deposits the employee FICA taxes and notifies the actual employer of the amount of compensation paid, the responsibility for the employer portion of FICA taxes can be transferred back to the actual employer). Also, disability payments paid directly by the state or third party sick pay that comes from premiums paid by the employee are not taxable -- unless the premium contributions were made as part of a pre-tax cafeteria plan (where taxes were deferred). Sick pay does not include workers' compensation payments, disability retirement payments, medical expense payments or payments not related to absence from work. For further information about sick pay and sick pay plans, look at IRS Publication 15-A (Employer's Supplemental Tax Guide).

Note: Only the first six months of sick pay (following the employee's last day of work) are FICA taxable; however any return to work - even for a day - starts a new six-month period.

Note 2: Any portion of the sick pay attributable to after-tax deductions from the employee's pay are not subject to Social Security, Medicare or FUTA tax. For example if the employee paid for 20% of the plan cost through after-tax payroll deductions, then 20% of the sick pay benefits are non-taxable for Social Security, Medicare or FUTA purposes.

Q: **What if an employee being paid sick pay by a 3rd party provider wants federal income tax withheld from those payments?**
A: An employee can fill out a Form W-4S (Request for Federal Income Tax Withholding From Sick Pay) to authorize the 3rd party payer to withhold federal income tax. If the 3rd party provider agrees to withhold taxes the provider is liable for withholding the employee's share of Social

Security and Medicare tax as well as the employee's federal income tax (the provider is also responsible for the employer share of FICA and FUTA tax unless an agreement has been made transferring that responsibility back to the employer).

Q: **What is the Federal Family and Medical Leave Act (FMLA)?**
A: Sick pay is strictly voluntary for employers; however under the terms of the Federal Family and Medical Leave Act of 1993, employees may be entitled to take leave to care for themselves or for certain family members without losing their job or benefits. The FMLA provides for up to 12 weeks of unpaid leave for employees with a family or medical emergency who work for a company with 50 or more employees within a 75 mile radius. The leave may be used all at one time or in separate days, weeks, or hours (however the leave must be taken within 12 months of the childbirth, adoption, illness or other qualifying event).

Q: **Can an employer dock an exempt, salaried employee's wages for sick days missed?**
A: An exempt salaried employee can't be docked for sick days missed unless the employer has a valid sick pay plan in place that offers at least five sick days per year. Even then, a person can only be docked for missing a full day -- not for a partial day. However, the employer is not required to pay full salary for weeks in which an exempt employee takes unpaid leave under the Federal Family and Medical Leave Act.

Q: **What is "disability insurance"?**
A: Disability insurance covers situations where an employee is injured on the job or suffers a job-related illness and needs at least a portion of their normal income while they're unable to work. Employers can choose to pay for short term and long term disability coverage, let the employee pay for the coverage, or share the cost of coverage with the employee. If you, the employer, pay the premiums, your employees aren't taxed on the premium amount (IRS Code Section 106). Under IRS Code Section 125, if you choose to make the employees pay the premiums, they pay the premiums on a pre-tax basis through payroll deductions. In turn, employees would be able to collect disability tax-free if they qualified for disability.

Q: **What is a "short term disability policy"?**
A: Short term disability insurance policies pay a percentage of an ill or injured employee's salary for a specified amount of time if he can't perform his duties on the job. Coverage usually starts within 14 days after the employee suffers the injury or illness. Short term disability plans usually set out certain conditions that the employee has to meet to

qualify for coverage, such as the employee needs to have worked for the company for a certain length of time prior to the injury or illness and the employee needs to work full-time (usually 30 hours or more a week). Benefits normally cover 50% to 70% of the person's weekly pay and last between 10 and 26 weeks (6 months). Some states such as New Jersey, New York, Rhode Island, and Hawaii mandate that short term disability benefits have to be provided for up to 26 weeks.

Q: **What is "long term disability insurance"?**
A: Some employers provide long term disability insurance, which kicks in when short term disability payments end. Typically, long term benefits provide a percentage of the disabled employee's pay (50% of base salary for example) until the employee turns 65.

Earned Income Credit

Advance payments of the Earned Income Tax Credit can no longer be made through payroll after December 31, 2010. However employers are still required to notify employees who have no income tax withheld that they may be able to claim a refund because of the EIC. To do so, use IRS Notice 797 or an equivalent form. Note: The paragraphs below are for reference only.

Q: What is "Advance payment of Earned Income Tax Credit"?
A: The Earned Income Credit is a tax credit for employees whose annual income is under a certain level ($33, 241 for 2007 if filing single or $35,241 if married filing jointly). There are a number of rules governing eligibility for the EIC -- IRS Publication 596 explains what's required. If an employee of yours determines that he's eligible he can elect to get advance payments of a portion of the tax credit on each paycheck rather than waiting till the end of the year. To do so, he can fill out a Form W-5 and give you the lower portion of the form (Note: if an employee is married and his or her spouse also works, each spouse should file a separate W-5). An EIC payment is not subject to income, Social Security or Medicare taxes (see "Payroll Taxes") -- it's simply added to the employee's net pay.

Q: How do I calculate EIC payment amounts -- and where does the money come from?
A: You'll find a set of EIC payment tables in your Circular E (IRS Publication 15) -- notice that there are separate tables depending on whether or not there's a spouse who has also filed a Form W-5. As to where the money comes from, the advance EIC payments are really a tax credit from IRS, so the employer simply reduces the amount of his payroll tax deposit by the total of EIC payments. In other words, if you paid out $200 in EIC payments, you would reduce the amount of your income tax, Social Security, or Medicare deposit amount by $200 (the EIC total will be counted by IRS as part of your tax deposit).

Employee and Employer Taxes

Q: **What taxes does the employee pay?**
A: Generally, an employer withholds the following taxes from each employee's paycheck: Social Security, Medicare, federal income tax, and (depending on the state) state income tax and state disability tax. If you have employees in Alaska, New Jersey, or Pennsylvania, you will also have to withhold some state unemployment tax from your employees' wages and (in the case of New Jersey) Family Leave tax. In addition there may be local taxes that have to be withheld.

Q: **What are Social Security and Medicare taxes and how are they calculated?**
A: Social Security and Medicare taxes are components of the Federal Insurance Contributions Act (or FICA). Social Security tax provides funding for retirement income, survivor benefits and disability insurance. Medicare provides health insurance for people 65 and older (and some people under 65 with disabilities). Normally Social Security tax is calculated as 6.2% of the employee's FICA taxable wages and the employer pays an equal matching amount. For 2011 and 2012 the employee's Social Security tax rate was reduced to 4.2% but that rate returned to the normal 6.2% in 2013. Social Security withholding stops when FICA taxable wages reach the current year maximum wage limit ($118.500 for 20165). Medicare is calculated as 1.45% of FICA taxable wages and, as with Social Security, is matched by an equal employer contribution. There is no wage limit on Medicare withholding, so it continues all year.

For 2013 and beyond there is also an additional Medicare withholding amount that kicks in when an employee's taxable earnings exceed $200,000 – from that point on, the Medicare withholding rate goes up to 2.35% of FICA taxable wages (the law actually states that the Medicare rate goes up when a single person's wages exceeds $200,000 or a married person's wages exceeds $250,000 – however for payroll purposes all employees can be considered single in determining when to start the additional Medicare withholding and married individuals can recover the overpayment of Medicare tax on their annual tax return). The additional Medicare tax on wages over $200,000 applies only to the employee – there is no employer match.

Note: Wages that are deducted for certain pre-tax benefit plans (such as Section 125 Cafeteria plans) are (usually) not FICA taxable, which means that an employee's FICA taxable wages are not necessarily equal to his or her total wages.

Q: **How do I calculate FIT (Federal Income Tax)?**
A: If you do your payroll manually in-house, you will need a copy of the wage bracket tables issued by IRS. These tables are included in IRS Publication 15 (also known as the "Circular E") which is normally mailed to every employer at the beginning of the year. If you don't receive a Circular E in the mail you can download a copy from the IRS website at www.irs.gov. To figure the withholding tax for a given employee, you have to look at the marital status and number of exemptions claimed on that person's W-4 -- then go the appropriate table for your pay period (weekly, bi-weekly, etc.) and for that employee's marital status (single or married). Then find the row in the table that includes the employee's gross pay and the column in that row for the number of exemptions being claimed, and use the withholding tax shown there. If an employee's wages are greater than the last amount listed in the wage bracket table you will need to use the percentage withholding tables (also in the Circular E).

Q: **How do I calculate state withholding tax?**
A: Assuming you're not operating in one of the nine states that have no state withholding tax, the process of figuring state withholding is similar to calculating federal withholding. Most states have a set of tax tables which work the same way as the federal tables, although in some cases there may be an additional calculation or two, such as subtracting a "standard deduction" amount from gross pay along with the deduction for the number of exemptions claimed. Also, a few states have a different method of calculating withholding tax, such as simply multiplying federal withholding by a certain percentage. You can check on the exact method used in your state by contacting the appropriate state agency.

Q: **What if I have employees who live in one state and work in a different state?**
A: Almost all states that have a personal income tax require that anyone working there, including non-residents, pay tax on the income earned in that state. In general non-resident employees who work in a state that has a personal income tax have state tax withheld in that state. At the end of the year those employees have to file a tax return with the state where they work and with the state where they reside. They get credit in their home state for the state tax paid where they work but if their home state has a higher income tax rate they have to pay the difference to their home state.

To avoid this double burden some states have reciprocal tax agreements with other states. If two states have a reciprocal agreement and an employee lives in one of those states and works in the other, he or she will only be subject to income tax in the state where he or she lives. Employers are not required to withhold tax for the state where the employee lives, but many employers will establish an account with a reciprocal state and withhold the tax for the employee's state of residence. Almost all states that have state tax reciprocal agreements have a form that an employee can complete that will make his income exempt from withholding tax in the state where he works.

Here is a list of states with reciprocal agreements, the reciprocating state or states, and the form the employee needs to fill out:
- District of Columbia – Any other state - Form D4-A
- Illinois – Iowa, Kentucky, Michigan, and Wisconsin - Form IL-W-5-NR
- Indiana – Kentucky, Michigan, Ohio, Pennsylvania, and Wisconsin - Form WH-47
- Iowa – Illinois - Form 44-016
- Kentucky – Illinois, Indiana, Michigan, Ohio, Virginia, West Virginia, and Wisconsin - Form 42A809
- Maryland – District of Columbia, Pennsylvania, Virginia, and West Virginia - Form MW 507
- Michigan – Illinois, Indiana, Kentucky, Minnesota, Ohio, and Wisconsin - Form MI-W4
- Minnesota – Michigan and North Dakota - Form MWR
- Montana – North Dakota – Form NR-2
- New Jersey – Pennsylvania – Form NJ-165
- North Dakota – Minnesota and Montana – Form NDW-R
- Ohio – Indiana, Kentucky, Michigan, Pennsylvania, and West Virginia – Form IT-4NR
- Pennsylvania – Indiana, Maryland, New Jersey, Ohio, Virginia, and West Virginia – Form REV-420
- Virginia – District of Columbia, Kentucky, Maryland, Pennsylvania, and West Virginia – Form VA-4
- West Virginia – Kentucky, Maryland, Ohio, Pennsylvania, and Virginia – Form WV/IT-104R
- Wisconsin – Illinois, Indiana, Kentucky, and Michigan – Form W-220.

Q: **As an employer do I have to pay taxes?**
A: Federal law levies certain payroll taxes on employers and you are considered to be an employer if you paid wages of $1,500 or more during any calendar quarter in the current or previous calendar year or if you

employed one or more persons on at least some portion of one day in each of 20 or more calendar weeks during the current or previous calendar year.

Q: **What taxes does the employer pay?**
A: An employer is required to match the Social Security and Medicare taxes withheld from employee paychecks. You also have to pay federal unemployment (FUTA) taxes up to a maximum wage limit per employee of $7000 and state unemployment (SUTA) taxes up to whatever the SUI (state unemployment insurance) wage limit is in your state. There may also be additional taxes such as disability or family leave tax, depending on the state or states where you operate.

Q: **Which states have disability taxes?**
A: California, Hawaii, New Jersey, New York, Rhode Island (and Puerto Rico) all have disability insurance taxes,

Q: **Is an owner or a partner in a company subject to withholding taxes?**
A: In general an owner or partner is not considered an employee and is not subject to withholding taxes. However in some cases if a person has other partners who can control his wages and have the power to fire him, he may be considered an employee of the company.

Q: **At what point in the pay period do I become liable for the payroll taxes withheld?**
A: Your tax liability starts on the date you pay your employees, regardless of when they did the work being paid for on that paycheck. For example, if a pay period runs from September 16 through September 30 and you date the checks October 4, your tax liability begins on the 4th of October.

Q: **What is FUTA tax and how does it work?**
A: FUTA (the Federal Unemployment Tax Act) collects taxes from employers to administer the unemployment compensation program that provides payments to employees who have lost their jobs. The current FUTA tax rate is 6.0% and applies to the first $7000 in FUTA taxable earnings for each employee. Each state also has a State Unemployment Tax (SUTA) and employers who pay their state unemployment tax on a timely basis can take a 5.4% credit against their FUTA rate, leaving a net FUTA rate of .6% (or 0.006). FUTA tax is calculated every quarter by multiplying .006 times each employee's wages for the quarter (but only on the first $7000 in wages for each person). If the tax is $500 or less at the end of a quarter you are not required to make a deposit; however,

you must add it to the tax for the next quarter. FUTA tax is due by the last day of the month following the end of the quarter (for example, first quarter deposits are due on April 30th -- unless that day is a holiday, in which case tax is due on the next working day). Certain types of employees are exempt from FUTA tax, including:

- People who perform services outside of the United States
- Newspaper carriers under 18 years of age
- People working for 501(c)(3) non-profit organizations
- Children under 21 employed by parent(s)
- General or limited partners of a partnership
- Hospital interns

Note: If there are any states that borrowed money from the federal government during the year to pay unemployment benefits and failed to repay all the money they borrowed, they are designated by the Department of Labor as "credit reduction" states. Employers in those states must reduce their .054 credit on Form 940 by a specified "reduction rate". The exact amount of the credit reduction is computed by filling out Schedule A of Form 940 and any additional money owed for credit reduction must be included in the fourth quarter FUTA deposit. For 2016 California was the only credit reduction state, with a reduction rate of 1.8%..

Q: Are U.S. citizens working in a foreign country subject to FUTA tax?

A: Yes, if the work they're doing would be subject to FUTA if it was being performed in the U.S.

Q: What is SUTA tax and how does it work?

A: Under SUTA (the State Unemployment Tax Act), each state has its own unemployment compensation program funded primarily by taxes on employers. With the exception of Alaska, New Jersey, and Pennsylvania, state unemployment taxes are collected from employers only and no taxes are withheld from employees. To calculate the amount of SUI (state unemployment insurance) taxes you owe for a given calendar quarter you simply multiply the total SUI wages paid to your employees in that quarter times the SUI rate assigned to you by the state. Each state sets a limit on the wages that you have to pay SUI tax on for any one employee, so you only include the employee's wages up to that limit when you calculate the amount of SUI tax you owe.

Q: If I hire someone in mid-year do I need to take into account his FUTA and SUTA contributions in his previous job?

A: No, Federal Unemployment Tax (FUTA) and State Unemployment

Tax (SUTA) start over again when someone takes a job with a new employer. The new employer is responsible for withholding FUTA up to the current $7,000 limit and state unemployment tax up to that state's current SUI (state unemployment insurance) wage limit.

Q: What if a new employee has already met the Social Security limit with a previous employer?
A: Regardless of how much the person has had withheld previously during the year, Social Security withholding starts from zero again with a new employer. If the employee is over-withheld at the end of the year he can get a refund on his individual tax return. The employer however is simply out the amount of the employer match on Social Security and isn't eligible for any type of refund.

Q: If an employee is already receiving Social Security benefits do I still withhold FICA?
A: Yes, employees are not exempted from FICA (Social Security and Medicare) taxes on the basis of age or the fact that they are receiving Social Security payments.

Q: Do I have to withhold taxes on non-cash items given to employees, like food, lodging or equipment?
A: Payments made in the form of food or lodging are generally taxable unless they are made in that form for the convenience of the employer and: (a) in the case of meals, they are provided on the business premises, and (b) in the case of lodging, the employee is required to accept lodging on the business premises as a condition of employment. Other forms of non-cash compensation are normally treated as taxable wages. Non-cash benefits should usually be valued at the "fair market value" for those items; i.e. the amount an individual would pay to an unrelated third party to obtain comparable benefits or property. The biggest problem with non-cash compensation is making sure you can collect the FICA and income taxes from the employee. If you also pay the employee cash wages, you can withhold all the required taxes from the cash portion of the compensation (provided there's enough money to cover all the taxes).

Q: Are employees of a non-profit organization subject to FICA taxes?
A: With the exception of ordained ministers, employees of non-profit organizations are subject to FICA taxes if they earn $100 or more per year.

Q: Are employees of a tax-exempt organization subject to federal

taxes?
A: Employees of tax-exempt organizations are subject to federal, state, and local taxes, including federal income tax withholding, FICA tax withholding, state income tax withholding, and federal and state unemployment taxes.

Q: **Do employees of a religious organization pay Social Security taxes?**
A: Some religious groups object to paying Social Security taxes and are allowed to choose not to participate in the Social Security program. They do not withhold those taxes from their employees' wages or pay the employer's matching share of Social Security taxes. Employees who work for religious organizations of this type must pay Social Security taxes if their earnings are more than $100 per year; in effect the employees are treated as if they were self-employed.

Q: **Do all states have a state income tax?**
A: No, there are currently nine states (Alaska, Florida, Nevada, South Dakota, Texas, Washington and Wyoming) that don't have an income tax. Accordingly, there is no state withholding tax for employees in those states.

Q: **What are "differential wages"?**
A: Differential wages are payments made by employers to employees who are on active military duty to make up the difference between their military pay and their normal pay. After 30 days the payments become subject to federal income tax withholding, but not FICA or FUTA withholding. In most cases federal withholding can simply be calculated as 25% of the wages paid.

Q: **Are there any special cases I should know about?**
A: If you're a sole proprietorship or a partnership and you hire your own children under age 18, you're not required to withhold Social Security or Medicare from their paychecks. Also, if your child is under 21, you aren't required to pay FUTA tax on his or her wages.

Tax Saving Tips for Employers and Employees

Q: **What are some payroll-related tax-saving strategies for me and my employees?**

A: Here are a few suggestions:

- 401(k) Plans – Employee contributions to 401(k) plans are tax-deferred so your employees pay federal and state withholding tax on the difference in pay after their 401(k) contribution is deducted.
- IRS Section 125 plans (also referred to as cafeteria or flex plans) allow employees to make tax-free contributions to an account which can be used to reimburse the employee for certain types of expenses. Since Section 125 plan contributions are exempt from Social Security and Medicare tax (as well as federal and state withholding), the employer also saves the cost of matching Social Security and Medicare taxes on those amounts.
  Note: Employees can select to make certain deductions under a Section 125 plan after-tax deductions, so that FICA and income taxes are withheld on those particular deductions.
- Flex plans can include options such as:
  - Flexible Spending Accounts – FSAs allow employees to contribute a portion of their pay (before taxes) to an account which can be used to pay for items such as over-the-counter medicines, eyeglasses or contacts, orthodontics, chiropractic care and other items not covered by another health plan. FSA funds can also be used to pay deductibles and co-payments, but not insurance premiums. The maximum contribution for 2016 is $2,550.
  - Health Savings Accounts – HSAs allow employees to put part of their pay into a special account - either to save for future medical expenses or to pay for current expenses not covered by another health plan (employers may also contribute to HSAs). In order to contribute to an HSA the employee must be covered by an IRS qualified high-deductible health plan. Unlike FSAs unused funds in an HSA can be carried forward to a new year and can also be taken with the employee if he or she switches jobs.
  - Dependent Care Assistance – Flex plans can include the option for employees to set aside part of their income (tax-free) to pay for day care expenses for children under age 13.
  - Premium Only Plans (POP) - POP plans allow employees to elect to withhold a portion of their pre-tax salary to pay their

premium contribution for most employer-sponsored health and welfare benefit plans. Premiums may include the employee's share of employer-sponsored health, dental, accident, disability and group-term life insurance.

Employers save the cost of matching Social Security and Medicare taxes on the pre-tax amounts contributed to flex plans by employees. In addition, employer contributions to retirement plans and workers' comp insurance may also be reduced since they're based on lower taxable wages.

Timekeeping

Q: **What are the disadvantages of a manual timekeeping system?**
A; There are three main disadvantages of keeping time card data manually:
1) Time spent in preparing time cards by hand (including time spent in verifying the information and figuring shift and department totals).
2) Human error in collecting and posting the time card data.
3) Incorrect or missing time cards, as well as intentional "fudging" of time card information.

Q: **What type of features are included in automated timekeeping systems?**
A: Automated timekeeping systems offer features such as:
- Clock in/clock out by swiping a card through a card reader.
- Biometric scan capability to prevent "buddy punching".
- Automatically transferring time clock data to the payroll database.
- Clock in/clock out over a local network or over the Internet.
- Allowing employees to view their time card data online.
- Employee scheduling.
- Automatic lunch time deductions.
- Automatic overtime calculations.
- Holiday scheduling.
- The ability to see at a glance who is in and who is clocked out.
- Detail and summary time card reports and editing capability.

Q: **How do biometric time clocks work?**
A: Instead of using a code or key of some type biometric time clocks have each employee's hand print, finger print, retina pattern or some other physical feature scanned into the system and match that to the employee when a worker clocks in or out.

Q: **What if we want to install a PC based timeclock system but not all employees have access to a PC?**
A: Many time clock systems have the ability to add remote terminals or mobile devices that allow employees to clock in and clock out without using a PC.

Q: **I have an employee who clocks in early at 7 AM but his shift doesn't start until 8 AM – do I have to pay him for the extra hour?**

A: Yes, the Fair Labor Standards Act (FLSA) requires that an employer pay employees for all time on the job. Rather than not paying him for the extra hour, issue a written warning to all employees about clocking in early and if he continues to do so then fine him for violating company policy.

Q: **Can I require salaried employees to clock in and out?**
A: As long as the policy applies to all employees salaried workers can be required to clock in and out along with hourly employees. Note: Having salaried employees record their time in and out can help prevent lost time due to extra long lunch hours or other unaccounted for time away from the job.

Calculating Pay Checks

Q: **What if I need to convert a bi-weekly pay rate to an hourly rate?**
A: To convert a per pay period rate to an hourly pay rate:
- For a weekly payroll divide the weekly pay rate by the number of hours in a standard work week (for example, if you pay someone $500 per week and the standard work week is 40 hours the hourly pay rate is $500 divided by 40 hours or $12.50 per hour).
- For a bi-weekly payroll divide the bi-weekly pay rate by 2, then divide the result by the number of hours in a standard workweek.
- For a semi-monthly payroll multiply the semi-monthly rate times 24 (the number of pay periods in a year), divide by 52 (the number of weeks in a year) and divide the result by the number of hours in a standard work week (40) to get the hourly pay rate.
- For a monthly payroll follow the same steps as for a semi-monthly payroll, but multiply the monthly pay rate by 12.

Q: **How do I figure an hourly rate for an employee who is paid according to the number of pieces he produced during the week?**
A: To calculate an hourly rate for a pieceworker add the total earnings from what was paid for the pieces produced plus any other pay and divide by the number of hours worked during the week.

Q: **Is there an easy, free way to figure paycheck amounts by hand?**
A: If you figure paychecks manually you may be able to use one of these free online calculators:
- http://www.paycheckcity.com – Offers standard (salary and hourly) calculators as well as specialized versions (gross up, 401(k), bonus-%, and bonus-aggregate).
- http://www.adp.com/tools-and-resources/calculators-and-tools.aspx – Includes several different types of pay calculators.
- http://www.paycycle.com/external/business/paycheckCalculators.jsp – Includes hourly, salary and gross-to-net calculators.

All of the above web-based calculators offer the ability to select the pay frequency, the state for which state taxes are to be withheld, and the option to enter multiple voluntary deductions any of which can be marked as exempt from FICA, federal, or state tax.

Q: **What if I want to print the paychecks I calculated?**
A: If you want to print actual paychecks one option is:
  http://www.paycheckmanager.com

Their free payroll calculator computes federal and state withholding, and provides for 401k, 125 plan, local taxes and other special deductions. You can also enter "year-to-date" information to ensure the accuracy of certain tax calculations (such as Social Security tax). You will also have to enter your bank information including the bank routing number and your account number. Once you have entered all the paycheck information you can download a PDF file containing the check images. To print the checks you have to open the PDF file in Adobe Reader and print it on a laser printer, using standard 3-part blank check stock. The MICR coding (the funny looking characters at the bottom of the check) contains the routing and account numbers - in order for the bank to be able to scan it properly you may also have to use a special MICR toner cartridge in your printer. **Note:** None of your information is saved after you leave the website so you have to enter your setup information each time you do payroll (to save your data you have to pay for their Payroll Manager service).

Payroll Tax Deposits

Q: **What payroll taxes do I need to deposit?**
A: You need to deposit the Social Security tax, Medicare tax and federal income tax withheld from your employees' wages plus your employer match amount (equal to the total of the Social Security and Medicare taxes). That amount makes up your 941 tax deposit and is deposited monthly or semiweekly. You also need to make a quarterly deposit of your 940 or FUTA (Federal Unemployment Tax Act) taxes, equal to 6.0% of the federal taxable wages (up to a limit of $7,000 of taxable wages) paid to your employees during the quarter. Normally you can take a 5.4% credit against your FUTA tax for SUTA (State Unemployment Tax Act) contributions made to the state, which reduces your FUTA deposit to 0.6% of the employees' taxable wages for the quarter (you may have to make an additional FUTA payment at the end of the year if any state where you do business is a "credit reduction" state – a state which has borrowed more in unemployment funds from the federal government than it has paid back). You also need to make quarterly SUI (state unemployment insurance) tax deposits to your state (contact your state unemployment agency for detailed information on making SUTA deposits). Note: A few states also have SDI (disability insurance) and/or workers compensation taxes that are collected through payroll.

Q: **How do I handle making tax deposits?**
A: It's a good idea to set up a separate bank account just for payroll transactions; then you simply make your tax deposits (Social Security, Medicare and federal income tax) from your payroll account. All employers are required to use the Electronic Federal Tax Payment System (EFTPS) to make their payroll tax deposits. You can initiate your deposit by calling the information in by phone or by entering it over the Internet.

Q: **How often do I need to make payroll tax deposits?**
A: When you make your deposit depends on the total tax liability you've reported on your Form 941 (Employer's Quarterly Tax Return) during a four-quarter "lookback" period. The deposit schedule is based on your total taxes during those four quarters: if you reported more than $50,000 in total taxes during the period from July 1st of 2 years ago to June 30th of last year you must make tax deposits on a semi-weekly basis; if less than $50,000 you can make monthly deposits (all new employers make monthly deposits for the first calendar year). If you have a total tax liability of less than $2500 per quarter then you can simply send your tax payment in with your Form 941. For semi-weekly depositors, if your pay

date falls on Wednesday through Friday make your deposit by the following Wednesday; for pay dates that fall on Saturday through Tuesday, make your deposit by the following Friday.

Q: **Are there any exceptions to the above rules?**
A: Regardless of your normal payment schedule, if you accumulate a tax liability of $100,000 or more on any day during a deposit period, you have to deposit the tax by the next working day (this is the so-called "One Day" rule). Once you accumulate a deposit of $100,000 or more you automatically become a semi-weekly depositor for the remainder of the current year and for the following year. Also, if you write a manual check and date it in the middle of a pay period, the standard rules for depositing the taxes withheld still apply; if you're on a semiweekly schedule you need to deposit the taxes from the manual check based on the check date.

Q: **Can I be penalized for failure to follow the above rules?**
A: Yes. If you fail to make the required payments on time IRS can impose penalties ranging from 2% of the amount due for payments one to five days late to 15% for amounts not paid within ten days after receiving a notice from IRS.

Q: **What is the "safe harbor" rule for payroll tax deposits?**
A: If you deposit a small amount less than your full tax deposit liability, IRS will forgo any penalties if:
- The amount of the shortfall isn't more than the greater of $100 or 2% of the entire amount due
- The deposit you made was made on time
- You deposit the shortfall amount by the appropriate make-up date (the make-up date for monthly depositors is the due date for the 941 quarterly return and the make-up date for semiweekly depositors is the first Wednesday or Friday, whichever is earlier, falling on or after the 15th day of the month following the month in which the deposit was due)

Q: **What if I need to make a deposit and don't have an EIN yet?**
A: If you have applied for an EIN (Employer Identification Number) but haven't received it yet and need to make a payroll tax deposit, make the check for the taxes payable to "United States Treasury" and mail it along with an explanation to the IRS office where you would normally send your Form 941 (Employer's Quarterly Tax Return). IRS addresses are on the Form 941 or you can find them at www.irs.gov. Be sure to use the "without a payment" mailing address.

Q: **What if I want to appoint an agent to make our tax deposits?**
A: You can file IRS form 2678 (Employer/Payer Appointment of Agent) to request to have an agent file information returns and make tax deposits for you.

Pre-Tax Deductions and Fringe Benefits

Q: **What are "Pre-Tax Deductions"?**
A: Pre-tax deductions are subtracted from an employee's gross pay (and from his or her taxable gross) before any taxes are calculated, decreasing the amount of tax taken out of the paycheck. Cafeteria (so-called "Plan 125") deductions reduce the employee's taxable gross, which means less tax for the employee and less for the employer (because the Social Security and Medicare match is reduced as well). Other examples of pre-tax deductions are amounts withheld for Flexible-Spending Accounts, Health Savings Accounts, and Archer Medical Savings Accounts.

Q: **What are "Tax deferred deductions"?**
A: Tax deferred deductions (or "tax deferred benefits") are excluded from federal income tax (and normally from state income tax), although Social Security and Medicare taxes are still paid. Simple IRAs and 401(k) plans are examples of tax deferred deductions.

Q: **What are "defined benefit" and "defined contribution" pension plans?**
A: There are two general types of pension plans – defined benefit plans and defined contribution plans. A defined benefit plan promises participants a specified monthly benefit at retirement. The benefit may be stated as a flat dollar amount such as $500 per month or the benefit may be calculated through a formula that takes into account factors such as salary and years of service. A defined contribution plan doesn't promise a specified amount at retirement. In defined contribution plans the employer or the participant (or both) contribute to the employee's individual account and these contributions are invested on the participant's behalf. The participant will eventually receive whatever the balance is in their account. Defined contribution plans include 401(k) plans, 403(b) plans, employee stock ownership plans, and profit-sharing plans. The general rules of ERISA (the Employment Retirement Income Security Act) apply to all of these types of plans.

Note: Both types of plans described above are considered "qualified" compensation plans under IRS regulations and employer expenses associated with those plans can be deducted from the company's income. Employers may also set up "non-qualified" tax-deferred plans (which can include deferred compensation, executive bonuses, and split-dollar insurance) for key executives or other select employees. Expenses associated with non-qualified plans cannot be deducted from the company's income until the money is actually paid out to the individual participants but it can still provide tax-deferred income to the employees in the plan.

Q: What is a 401(k) plan and how does it work?

A: 401(k) plans are employer sponsored retirement plans which let an employee save for retirement while deferring income taxes on the money put into the plan until the funds are eventually withdrawn. As mentioned above, employee 401(k) plan contributions are exempt from federal income tax but not from FICA taxes (Social Security and Medicare). Each employee can elect to have a certain amount (or a percentage of earnings) paid into his or her 401(k) account. In most 401(k) plans the employee can select from a number of different investment options (mostly mutual funds) and divide his contribution amount among those options. In addition employers can contribute matching funds (usually a percentage of the employee contribution) and employer contributions are tax-free. Details concerning topics such as the amount of the employer match and whether 401(k) amounts are taken on bonus checks vary with the particular 401(k) plan involved. There is a maximum amount that an employee can elect to defer during the year. The 2016 limit is $18,000 per year, although employees age 50 or over may be eligible to contribute up to $24,000 under a "catch-up" provision. When an employee leaves, the 401(k) plan generally remains active for the rest of the employee's life (although funds have to begin to be drawn out by April 1st of the year following the date when the employee reaches the age of 70 1/2).

Q. What are Roth 401(k) plans?

A: Effective January 1, 2006, 401(k) participants have the option of allocating part or all of their contributions to a separate Roth account (generally known as a Roth 401(k)). In contrast to normal 401(k) contributions which are not taxed until the money is withdrawn, contributions to a Roth 401(k) are taxed when the contribution is made and distributions are tax-free.

Q: When must an employer deposit withheld employee pension plan contributions into the plan?

A: Employers must transmit employee contributions no later than the 15th business day of the month immediately after the month in which the contributions were withheld.

Q: What is a 403(b) plan?

A: 403(b) retirement plans are similar to a 401(k) plan, but are limited to certain public school employees, employees of tax-exempt organizations, and ministers. The limit on additions to a 403(b) plan for 2016 (the combination of employer contributions and employee contributions by means of a salary reduction agreement) is $18,000, with an additional "catch-up" contribution limit of $6,000 for employees aged 50 and over.

Q: **What is a Traditional Individual Retirement Account (IRA)?**
A: An individual account or annuity set up with a financial institution such as a bank or mutual fund company. Individuals can put personal savings in the account (up to a certain annual limit) and the money in the account grows, tax deferred. However, distributions from a traditional IRA are subject to federal and state taxes – and distributions prior to age 59 ½ are also subject to a 10% penalty. You may be able to avoid the early withdrawal penalty under the following circumstances:
- A first-time home purchase
- Death or disability
- Qualified educational expenses
- Unreimbursed medical expenses
- Health insurance if you're unemployed

After age 59 ½ distributions are penalty free – and starting at age 70 ½ traditional IRA owners must begin making withdrawals from their accounts or incur severe penalties.

Q: **What is a Roth Individual Retirement Account?**
A: A Roth IRA is basically the same as a traditional IRA except that it's not tax deferred – federal and state taxes are paid up front on the money placed in a Roth IRA. Contributions do not have to stop at age 70 ½ and qualified distributions for a Roth IRA are tax-free and penalty-free provided that five years have passed since the IRA was established and that one of the following conditions applies:
- Over age 59 ½
- Death or disability
- First-time home purchase

Q: **What are Simplified Employee Pension plans (SEPs)?**
A: Any employer may sponsor a simplified employee pension plan or SEP (generally referred to as an SEP IRA). Participating employees have to set up an individual retirement account or IRA - then the employer can make flat dollar amount contributions to the employee's IRA or percentage contributions of up to 25 percent of the person's annual compensation. For 2016, the flat dollar amount limit is $53,000 or 25% of the employee's salary (up to a maximum of $260,000 of salary, whichever is smaller). Employees can also contribute to their SEP IRA if the plan allows non-SEP contributions (although the amount the employee can deduct on his or her tax return for IRA contributions may

be reduced by the the employee's participation in the SEP plan). SEP plans have to be available to all employees who are at least 21 years old, have earned at least $450 and who have worked for the company for three of the preceding five years. Employers have the option of offering the plan to even more employees – those who have worked for the company for over a year for example. The employer can deduct all of the contributions made to the plan as a business expense and the money is not considered to be taxable income to the employees until they take withdrawals from their account (investment earnings are also tax-deferred).

Q: **Are employer contributions to an SEP taxable to the participating employees?**
A: No, employer contributions to SEP-IRAs are not included in their gross income (except for excess contributions).

Q: **Do contributions have to be made to an SEP every year?**
A: No, but if contributions are made to an SEP they have to be made to the SEP-IRAs of all participating employees.

Q: **How much of the contributions made to an SEP can be deducted on the business's tax return?**
A: A business can deduct the lesser of its contributions or 25% of employee compensation.

Q: **What is a Savings Incentive Match Plan for Employees (SIMPLE)?**
A: A SIMPLE plan (generally referred to as a Simple IRA) is a small business IRA-based retirement plan open to companies with 100 or fewer employees (and no other retirement plan in place). A Simple IRA is particularly attractive to employers because it requires fewer administrative fees and less paperwork than a 401(k) plan. Employees can choose whether or not to make regular contributions and the employer has the option of matching employee deferrals up to 3% of the person's annual salary or making non-elective contributions of 2% or less to all eligible employees. In either case, for 2016 employees can defer up to $18,000 (with employees 50 or older able to make "catch-up" contributions up to $3,000).

Q; **When do pension plan participants receive distributions after terminating their employment?**
A: Generally the law requires plans to pay retirement benefits no later than the time a participant reaches normal retirement age. However many plans, including 401(k) plans, provide for earlier payments under

certain circumstances – for example participants in a 401(k) plan may be eligible to receive payment of their proceeds once they have terminated employment.

Q: **What happens if a pension plan is terminated?**
A: If for some reason a pension plan has to be terminated the participants become 100 percent invested immediately upon plan termination, to whatever extent the plan is funded at that point.

Q: **What are Cafeteria plans?**
A: Cafeteria plans (also known as "Section 125" plans) allow employees to obtain tax-free medical coverage and insurance. Generally, qualified benefits under a cafeteria plan are not subject to FUTA, Social Security, Medicare or income tax withholding. However, if an employee elects to receive cash instead of a qualified benefit, that money is treated as regular taxable wages. Most cafeteria plans offer a basic set of benefits including health, dental and life insurance, sick leave or disability benefits, plus a secondary group of optional benefits. Employees are allocated a certain number of dollars to split among the various options available, with the dollar amounts provided by the employer normally being supplemented by employee pre-tax deductions. That way each employee is able to use pre-tax dollars to pay his or her portion of any insurance premiums, deductibles and coinsurance amounts under health benefit plans, or to pay medical bills which may not be covered by the employer's plan.

Q: **Exactly what benefits can be offered as part of a Cafeteria (Section 125) plan?**
A: A cafeteria plan can offer insured benefits (accident and health insurance, dental insurance, vision insurance, disability insurance, and group term life insurance) and non-insured benefits (dependent care assistance programs and medical/dental reimbursement for non-insured medical and dental expenses).

Q: **What benefits cannot be offered as part of a Section 125 plan?**
A: Medical Savings Accounts, dependent group term life insurance, and educational assistance.

Q: **How does a Cafeteria plan benefit the employer?**
A: The employer benefits from a Cafeteria plan in several ways. First of course, you don't have to pay matching FICA (Social Security and Medicare) tax or FUTA (federal unemployment) tax on the gross amount of employee pay "redirected" into the plan as cafeteria plan deductions. Then too, the employer may also participate in the plan to help pay for

uninsured medical expenses, dependent health premiums and dependent childcare. And, cafeteria plans can be a morale booster for your employees, removing some of the anxiety surrounding medical expense and health care issues.

Q: **Are there any drawbacks to participating in a Section 125 plan?**
A: Employees who select pre-tax benefits reduce their taxable income – but the fact that their taxable income is reduced also reduces benefits such as Social Security and retirement plans that are calculated based on taxable income.

Q: **Can everyone in the company participate in a Cafeteria plan?**
A: Sole proprietors, partners in a partnership and owners who own more than 2% of a subchapter S corporation cannot take part in a cafeteria plan.

Q: **Can an employee change his mind during the year as to which Cafeteria plan benefits he wants?**
A: Not in most cases; normally participants can only change their electives at the beginning of the plan year. However there are some plans that allow the employee to make changes at any time and even give the employees the ability to make changes online.

Q: **What happens if there's money left in a participant's account at the end of the plan year?**
A: The employee loses that money, so it's important that each employee makes a careful estimate of how much he or she needs to contribute to the plan each year.

Q: **What is a health reimbursement account (HRA)?**
A: HRAs are IRS sanctioned programs that allow an employer to set aside funds to reimburse medical expenses paid by participating employees. Health Reimbursement Accounts are started by the employer and administered by a third party or plan service provider. The employer decides if a credit balance in an employee's account may be rolled over from year to year and if so, how much rolls over. An HRA must be funded entirely by the employer and contributions cannot be paid through a voluntary salary reduction agreement (i.e., a cafeteria plan). There is no limit on an employer's contributions, which are excluded from an employee's income. Employees are reimbursed tax-free for qualified medical expenses up to a maximum dollar amount for a given coverage period. HRAs reimburse only those items agreed to by the employer which are not covered by the company's standard insurance plan.

Q: **What is an employee stock option (ESO)?**
A: Employers may offer certain employees the right to buy a specific number of shares of the company's stock during a time and at a price specified by the employer. The price the employer sets on the stock (called the "grant" or "strike" price) is discounted and is usually the current market price of the stock at the time the employee is given the options. If the company grows and performs well the price of the shares should go up and selling them will net the employees a profit, making stock options an incentive for employees to stay with the company.

Q: **What are "de minimus benefits"?**
A: de minimus or minimal benefits are items provided to employees that are of such little value that you can exclude them from the employee's wages. Cash and cash equivalents (such as use of a company credit card) can never be claimed as de minimus benefits, but there are numerous examples of items that do fit this classification: occasional use of a company copier, small inexpensive holiday gifts, occasional meals or movie tickets, etc. Group term life insurance benefits for the death of an employee's spouse or dependent also meet this requirement as long as the face amount of the policy is $2,000 or less. NOTE: IRS rules on de minimus items are not specific – in one case a $100 award was considered taxable, while in another case a $600 transfer of real estate proceeds was considered de minimus.

Q: **Are expense reimbursements subject to income tax withholding?**
A: Not if the expense reimbursement payments are made under an *accountable* plan. To qualify as an accountable plan the expense reimbursement arrangement has to meet three conditions:
- Expenses have to be business connected.
- Employee expenses need to be reported within a reasonable time period (normally 60 days).
- Over-payment of expenses need to be returned within a reasonable period (normally 120 days).

Q: **What exactly is a "per diem" allowance?**
A: Per Diem is an allowance paid to an employee for lodging, meals and incidental expenses that occur when traveling. Employers can use either a per diem rate for lodging and meals or for meals alone. Per diem payments are not part of an employee's wages if the payment is less than or equal to the federal per diem rate (available in IRS Publication 1542) and the employer receives an expense report from the employee. The expense report must include the business purpose of the trip, the date and place of the trip, and must be filed with the employer with 60

days. Note: Employers can pay more than the federal per diem rate, but the excess will be taxable to the employee.

Q: **Is employer-provided parking taxable?**
A: No – up to a limit of $230 per month.

Q: **I want to give one of our employees a fixed "vehicle allowance" amount to cover expenses on his personal car – what are the tax consequences?**
A: The vehicle allowance is treated as additional income to the employee and is taxable. It's up to the employee to keep track of his auto expenses and to claim them on his 1040 form. Note: the vehicle allowance must be paid on a regular basis (at least once per quarter).

Q: **Are stock bonuses considered taxable wages?**
A: Yes, stock bonuses are considered the same as wages.

Garnishments

Q: **What is a garnishment?**
A: A wage garnishment is a means of collecting a monetary judgment from a defendant by ordering a third party (the person's employer in our case) to pay a portion of the employee's earnings directly to the plaintiff. Title III of the Consumer Credit Protection Act (CCPA) limits the amount of an employee's earnings that may be garnished. Wage garnishments are normally limited to 25% of the employee's "disposable income" or whatever portion of the employee's wages are greater than thirty times the current federal minimum wage ($7.25 per hour), whichever is less. Garnishments can be taken for a number of reasons, but the most common ones are for child support or unpaid taxes. If an employee has multiple garnishments against his or her paycheck and there isn't enough money to satisfy all of them, the garnishments must be taken in order: federal first, then state or local, then any other judgments. If a state wage garnishment law differs from the federal law, the smaller garnishment must be used. Note that different states have varying laws concerning garnishments and you should check on the regulations in your particular state or states to make sure you are in compliance.

Note 1: In some cases involving child support or alimony, garnishments can be 50% or more of the employee's disposable income.
Note 2: In general, social security benefits, veteran's benefits, and railroad retirement benefits are not subject to garnishment.
Note 3: Garnishment restrictions do not apply to certain bankruptcy court orders or to amounts owed for federal or state taxes.
Note 4: Garnishment amounts are considered to be federal income taxable wages for the employee being garnished.

Q: **What are the restrictions on how wage garnishments are calculated?**
A: Garnishments are calculated based on the employee's "disposable earnings" which is the amount left over after all legally required deductions have been subtracted from earnings. Legally required deductions include Social Security and Medicare withholding taxes and federal, state and local income withholding taxes. They may also include withholding for an approved employee retirement plan. Once the disposable income has been determined multiply that amount by the garnishment rate to get the amount to be deducted.

Q: **Are tips considered to be wages when calculating a garnishment?**

A: Tips aren't generally considered disposable earnings when figuring the amount of a garnishment.

Q: **What is a "voluntary wage assignment"?**
A: A garnishment is a form of involuntary wage assignment. There are also voluntary wage assignments, where an employee specifically asks to have a portion of his or her wages deducted and paid to a third party to take care of things like loans, child support, or back taxes. Some loans also stipulate that if the employee falls behind in making payments that the payments are to be deducted from the employee's paycheck.

Q: **Which type of garnishment has precedence – a child support order or a tax levy?**
A: Child support orders have priority over federal tax levies (if the child support order was received first).

Q: **What are the priorities of the different types of garnishments?**
A: Child support orders have the highest priority (except as noted above), followed by bankruptcy orders, administrative garnishments for federal agencies, federal tax levies, state tax levies, local tax levies and creditor garnishments. (Note: the dollar limits on wage garnishments as mentioned above apply regardless of how many garnishments are levied against a given employee's wages).

Q: **How do I know if an employee's wages are subject to a federal tax levy?**
A: IRS will send you a copy of Form 668-W (Notice of Levy on Wages, Salary and Other Income) when a federal tax levy is to be enforced. Form 668-W includes instructions to the employer on withholding and submitting the levy amount.

Q: **Can I fire an employee who has received a garnishment order?**
A: The Consumer Credit Protection Act prohibits an employer from firing an employee whose earnings are subject to garnishment for any one debt – however, the Act doesn't prohibit firing an employee who is being garnished for two or more separate debts.

Net Pay

Q: **How do I figure an employee's net pay?**
A: Take the employee's gross pay and subtract Social Security withholding tax, Medicare tax, federal income tax and state income tax withholding. Then subtract any voluntary deductions (uniforms, health insurance, United Way, 401(k), etc.); that should give you the person's net pay. Keep in mind that certain other items can also affect net pay -- for example, if you pay auto allowances that add to a person's paycheck or if the employee has a garnishment.

Q: **What if an employee's deductions are more than his gross pay?**
A: If a worker's net pay winds up being negative, you have to start removing deductions (voluntary deductions first, then state withholding, federal withholding, and finally FICA taxes) until you reach zero net pay. Then you simply issue a voided, zero amount paycheck to that person.

Methods of Payment

Q: **Why should I consider paying my employees by direct deposit?**
A: There are a number of advantages (to both employer and employee) in using direct deposit. It saves the employer the cost of buying and printing checks, cuts down on paper handling, and - for companies with workers in different locations - eliminates the hassle of getting the paychecks to each location safely and on time. For the employee, it removes the worry of lost or stolen checks and the need to physically take his paycheck to the bank to get it deposited (especially if you're on vacation or out sick on payday).

Q: **How does direct deposit work?**

A: Direct deposit is a method of transferring your employees' net pay directly into their bank accounts without the need for issuing paychecks. You, the employer, contract with your bank for the bank to automatically transfer your employees' net pay into their accounts each payday. There is normally a set charge by the bank for this service (say $1 for each payroll transaction). Once your company has been approved for direct deposit you will need to supply the bank with the routing and account numbers for each of your employees who signs up for direct deposit. Then, when you run your payroll, there's something you need to be aware of -- normally there is a 2-day lead time for direct deposit. For instance, you need to have your ACH (direct deposit) file submitted to your bank on Wednesday to be sure that the employees pay will be in their bank accounts on Friday.

Q: **What's a transit number or routing number? And where can I find it?**
A: Each bank or similar financial institution has an identifying number (its ABA number) usually referred to as a "routing transit number" or just "routing number". If you look at a person's check you'll find both his bank's routing number and his bank account number printed in the MICR coding at the bottom of the check. The routing number should come first (reading from left to right), then the account number, and (usually) the check number on the far right.

Q: **What if an employee changes bank accounts?**
A: The employee needs to submit a new Direct Deposit Authorization so that his routing and/or account number can be changed before the next payday.

Q: **Can I require my employees to use direct deposit?**
A: It depends on the laws in your state -- most states require you to get written consent from the employee and make it clear that participation should be voluntary. However, there are a number of states do not have laws that specifically prohibit mandatory direct deposit programs, including Alabama, Illinois, Indiana, Iowa, Louisiana, Missouri, Tennessee, and Texas.

Q: **What are pay cards?**
A: Pay cards (or "Payroll debit cards") work a lot like regular direct deposit. Pay cards came into being primarily for those employees who don't have a bank account. Payroll debit cards offer the same type of advantages as direct deposit, except that the employee's pay is transferred to a special employer-created account that allows the employee to use his or her pay card in much the same way as you would a regular credit card.

Q: **What do I give to employees using direct deposit or pay cards in place of a check stub?**
A: You can print a "direct deposit advice" or "remittance advice" for each employee (or – with your employees' permission – you can email the remittance advice to them).

Self Employment Tax

Q: **What is "self-employment tax"?**
A: People who are in business but are not subject to withholding taxes (such as sole proprietors, members of a partnership, or independent contractors) are required to pay self-employment tax if they have an annual income of $400 or more. Self-employment taxes are basically the same as FICA taxes and, like FICA taxes, they consist of a Social Security tax and a Medicare tax. The total rate is normally 15.3 percent (12.4 percent for Social Security and 2.9 percent for Medicare). In other words the total self-employment tax is the same as if you added together the employee and employer portions of FICA tax due for a normal employee. Just as for a regular employee, the maximum amount of income subject to Social Security tax is $118,500 for 2016.

For sole proprietorships, partnerships, and limited-liability companies the self-employment taxes are imposed on your net self-employment income, which basically is just your business income minus your business deductions. The 15.3% multiplier is actually applied to 92.35% of the business's net earnings rather than 100% - the difference, 7.65%, is the amount that an employer would normally pay for you and would take as a business expense. To compute your self employment tax you can use the formula:
    12.4% x (.9235 x self-employment income) **or** 12.4% x $118,500 (whichever is less) + 2.9% x self-employment income

Q: **How do I report my self employment tax?**
A: You report self-employment taxes on your annual federal income tax return (on Schedule SE).

Q: **Do I need to make tax payments during the year?**
A: You are required to make quarterly estimated tax payments during the year (with each payment roughly equal to one fourth of the amount you expect to owe at the end of the year). Your quarterly payments are due on on the 15th of the month following the end of the quarter (or on the next business day if the 15th is a holiday or weekend). The simplest way to make your quarterly payments is through EFTPS (the Electronic Federal Tax Payment System).

Q: **What if I am self-employed and also an employee?**
A: If you are self-employed and also an employee of someone else, both incomes are included in order to determine the total amount of Social Security and Medicare tax that you need to pay. For example:

- You earned a salary of $38,100 from a job and have a net profit from Schedule C of $73,000.
- Your net earnings on Line 6 of Long Schedule SE are $67,416 ($73,000 x .9235).
- Subtract your salary of $38,100 from the maximum social security wage base of $118,500 and the result is $80,400.
- Of the two amounts, $67,416 and $80,400 multiply the social security rate of 12.4% (employee 6.2% and employer 6.2%) by the lower amount, $67,416.
- Your self employment tax is $10,314.64: 12.4% x $67,416 (social security tax) plus 2.9% x $67,416 (medicare tax).

Note: The net profit reported on Schedule C is carried to Schedule SE where it is reduced by 7.65% (the Schedule C net profit times .9235).

Q: **What if, at the end of the year, I've underpaid my estimated taxes?**
A: If you didn't pay enough tax during the year, either through withholding or by making estimated tax payments, you may have to pay a penalty. Generally, most taxpayers will avoid this penalty if they owe less than $1,000 in tax after subtracting any withholding and credits, or if they paid at least 90% of the tax for the current year, or 100% of the tax for the previous year, whichever is smaller.

Payroll Tax Reports and Record-Keeping

Q: **What reports do I need to file and when do I file them?**
A: At the end of every quarter most employers must file a Form 941 (Employer's Quarterly Tax Return) to report payroll withholding tax liabilities and payments. Semi-weekly depositors must also fill out and attach a Schedule B showing tax liability by date. In addition employers must submit whatever state reports are required (usually a summary of taxes withheld and a report covering state unemployment tax payments). Agricultural employers must file Form 943 quarterly instead of Form 941, while employers whose annual liability for social security, Medicare and federal income tax withheld is $1000 or less file Form 944 annually rather than submitting a Form 941 each quarter. Seasonal employers file Form 941 but don't have to file a report in quarters when they have no income. At the end of the year all employers have to file Forms W-3 and W-2 to report employee earnings, taxes and other information for the year, and Form 940 to report federal unemployment liability and payments. In addition employers should prepare a Form 1099-Misc for any non-employee (other than corporations) that you paid over $600 to during the year in rents, royalties, commissions, fees, prizes, or awards. Gross royalty payments of $10 or more must also be reported at year-end on a 1099-MISC.

Q: **What information goes on the Form 941 and Schedule B?**
A: Form 941 is used to report your quarterly withholding tax liability and tax payments for Social Security, Medicare, and federal income tax withholding, along with your employer matching payments for Social Security and Medicare. If your quarterly taxes are more than $2500 and you're a monthly depositor the tax total on line 10 should agree with the tax liability total on Part 2, line 15. If you're a semi-weekly depositor, you need to fill out Schedule B (a detailed listing of deposit liabilities by date) and the tax total on line 10 should agree with the total tax liability shown at the bottom of the Schedule B.
Note: Forms 941 and Schedule B can be downloaded form the IRS website at www.irs.gov.

Q: **What if I get a notice from IRS that there's a problem with my 941 and I want my payroll service to talk directly with IRS?**
A: If you want to have a third party (such as a payroll service or accountant) receive and discuss your tax information directly with IRS you can file IRS form 8821 (Tax Information Authorization). Power of Attorney and Declaration of Representative). You simply designate the tax period for which you are authorizing a third party to send and receive

information from IRS and the name of the third party. After the form is processed IRS will add the name of the third party designee to your account and that person will be authorized to discuss your tax account information. If you want to revoke a previously filed form 8821, write "Revoke" across the top of a copy of the previously filed form, sign your name and mail it to the same IRS office where you originally filed the form. You can also simply write a letter to IRS requesting to revoke the form 8821, listing the periods for which it is revoked and the tax matters for which it is revoked.

Q: **What if my company has a more serious problem and we want to appoint an agent to appear before IRS in our behalf?**
A: You can file Form 2848 (Power of Attorney and Declaration of Representative) to appoint an individual (someone knowledgeable about IRS regulations and someone you trust with your company's financial affairs) as your agent.

Q: **What is Form 944?**
A: Businesses with an annual payroll tax liability of $1,000 or less can file form 944 (Employer's Annual Federal Tax Return) at the end of the year rather than filing form 941 (Employer's Quarterly Federal Tax Return) each quarter. NOTE: If you file Form 944, you may NOT file Form 941. Normally IRS will notify you if you must file Form 944, but small businesses can also file a request with IRS to be allowed to file Form 944 instead of Form 941.

Q: **What information goes on the Form 940?**
A: Form 940 is the Employer's Annual Federal Unemployment Tax Act (FUTA) Tax Return. It lists the state where you pay unemployment (you'll need Form 940 Schedule A if you pay in more than one state), total payments to all employees, any payments that were exempt from FUTA tax (such as dependent care and group term life insurance), total of payments over and above the current $7000 FUTA wage limit, your FUTA tax liability (by quarter) and your FUTA tax deposited during the year. If you pay wages in a "credit reduction" state during 2016 you may also have to pay some additional FUTA tax by January 31, 2017. If your total tax liability for the year is under $100 you can simply send a check along with the form. Form 940 is normally due at the end of January -- however, if you made all of your deposits on time you have an additional 10 days to file your 940.

Q: **When do I have to have W-2 forms to my employees?**
A: You need to furnish a W-2 to each of your employees (including anyone who worked for you during the calendar year) by the end of

January of the following year. You also need to submit a W-3 and Copy A of your W-2 forms to Social Security by the end of February if filing paper forms or by the end of March if transmitting your W-2's electronically using the Social Security Administration's Business Services Online system.

Q: **Do I have to send copies of the W-2 forms to the state?**
A: The nine states that do not currently collect individual income tax (Alaska, Florida, Nevada, New Hampshire, South Dakota, Tennessee, Texas, Washington, and Wyoming) do not require employers to send copies of their W-2 forms. For all other states check with your state tax agency – some states require you to submit paper copies or file electronically, some states allow electronic filing only, and some states no longer require employers to submit W-2 copies at all.

Q: **Shouldn't the gross wages on a W-2 equal the employee's total wages for the year?**
A: Not necessarily. The wages shown in box 1 of the W-2 form are federal taxable wages only; if an employee has pre-tax benefits (such as cafeteria plan deductions) the person's annual wages will be reduced by the amount of those benefits.

Q: **What if I discover a wrong Social Security number on a W-2 and the W-2s have already been filed with the SSA?**
A: Fill out a W-2C form (available for download from www.irs.gov) – provide a copy to the employee and to the Social Security Administration. Ir you have signed up to use the Social Security Administration's BSO (Business Services Online) system you can also go to www.ssa.gov/employer and fill out and file W-2C forms electronically.

Q: **If I find out I have a wrong address on a W-2 what do I need to do?**
A: Issue the employee a new W-2 with the corrected address and mark it as a "Reissued W-2 Form" (do not send the revised copy A to the Social Security Administration).

Q: **What about reporting payments to independent contractors?**
A: If you pay an independent contractor more than $600 in a calendar year you're required to issue that contractor a Form 1099-Misc so that IRS can track tax payments by the contractor on that income.

Q: **What is Form 945?**
A: Form 945 (Annual Return of Withheld Federal Income Tax) is used to report withheld federal income tax from non-payroll payments, including:

pensions and backup withholding. The form can be downloaded directly from the IRS website.

Q: **How long do I need to keep payroll records?**
A: There are a number of (sometimes conflicting) guidelines on retention of payroll and human resource records. Generally speaking, records relating to a particular employee should be kept while the employee is with the company and for three years after he or she leaves. You're generally safe if you retain other payroll records for six years; beyond that you should probably consider shredding those records to dispose of them in a secure manner. Note: Most federal forms (such as 941, 940, W-3, W-2, and I-9 forms) can be disposed of after 4 years).

Q: **What is a "Certified Payroll" Report and why would I need one?**
A: If you are a contractor or subcontractor on a government-funded construction project you are required to submit weekly certified payroll reports to make sure you are complying with the terms of your government contract. The details of certified payroll reporting and what is required by different states is a complicated topic which is outside the scope of this book. For further information on exactly what reports you need to submit, you need to contact the appropriate state agency.

Basic Accounting Entries for Payroll

Q: What general journal entries do I make after a payroll has been run?

A: The first set of entries may look something like this:

	Debit	Credit
Hourly Wage expense	xxx	
Salaries expense	xxx	
Payroll tax expense	xxx	
Cash		xxx
Federal withholding taxes payable		xxx
Social security taxes payable		xxx
Medicare taxes payable		xxx
Federal unemployment taxes payable		xxx
State withholding taxes payable		xxx
State unemployment taxes payable		xxx
Garnishments payable		xxx

Plus any voluntary deduction expenses:

	Debit	Credit
401(k) contributions payable		xxx
Health insurance payable		xxx
(etc.)		

When the taxes and other liabilities are paid a second set of entries is made to relieve those payables:

	Debit	Credit
Cash		xxx
Federal withholding taxes payable	xxx	
Social security taxes payable	xxx	
Medicare taxes payable	xxx	
Federal unemployment taxes payable	xxx	
State withholding taxes payable	xxx	
State unemployment taxes payable	xxx	
Garnishments payable	xxx	
401(k) contributions payable	xxx	
Health insurance payable	xxx	

Payroll Software

Q: **Why use payroll software rather than doing payroll manually, letting an accountant do it, or using a payroll service bureau?**
A: In many cases one of the alternatives to in-house software may work fine for your company. Some reasons to consider using payroll software to process payroll in house are:

- An automated system can make entering and maintaining payroll data easier and may include edit checking to help eliminate keying and calculation errors.
- In-house payroll software allows you to protect employee personal information along with wage and salary information and it makes it easier to deal with last-minute payroll changes.
- Having your accountant handle your payroll along with your other accounting can be convenient – but your accountant may not be a payroll expert and today's payroll regulations are much more complicated than they were even a few years ago.
- Payroll service bureaus can be a very good choice, allowing you to spend more time on business operations – but they can also be somewhat expensive, you forfeit some control of your business, and you're dependent on the payroll service preparing your checks, direct deposits, tax and other reports on time.

Q: **What general features should I look for in a payroll software package?**
A: A comprehensive payroll package should include the ability to:

- Process payroll for employees in multiple states including state and local withholding tax calculations.
- Handle at least weekly, bi-weekly, semi-monthly and monthly pay frequencies.
- Pay salaried, hourly and piece-work employees.
- Handle multiple pay rates and shift differentials.
- Allow many different types of compensation such as regular pay, overtime, vacation, sick pay, commissions, bonuses, retro pay, dock (negative) pay, meals and tips.
- Accept data from time clock systems or provide an integrated time clock system.
- Provide for expense reimbursements.
- Do direct deposit payments (including pay cards) as well as checks.
- Print checks and deposit slips on blank laser stock and print signatures on checks.

- Handle various special types of deductions and benefits such as 401(k) contributions (pre-tax and Roth post-tax), 401(k) employer matching amounts, cafeteria plans, group term life insurance, IRAs, vehicle allowances and health savings accounts (HSAs).
- Create direct deposit files in standard NACHA (National Automated Clearing House Association) file format if necessary.
- Create either reports or electronic files needed to make federal payroll tax deposits through the Electronic Federal Tax Payment System (EFTPS), as well as state withholding tax and unemployment insurance tax deposits.
- Accrue and report various types of employee leave time (sick time, vacation, or personal time off).
- Provide reporting by cost center (department, store, property, etc.).
- Implement security features to protect your payroll data.
- Maintain detailed payroll history files.

Q: What are some desirable features to have in a payroll package?
A: Some features that would be nice to have include the ability for employees to have more direct access to their payroll information through web-based technology and direct entry of some data such as employee personal information by the employees.

Q: What's the best way to evaluate payroll software?
A: Look for software vendors who have been around for a while (as an indication that they have a relatively error-free package and that they will still be around in the future). And if at all possible arrange to get a live demo and a trial version of the software so that you can set up a few employees and run through some of your typical payrolls. That way you get a feel for how user-friendly the package is, how complete it is, and whether it can do everything you need it to do. Even if a package has the features you want, that doesn't mean that you'll like the way those features work – for example, you may be able to reverse and re-run a payroll but if it takes six steps and a half-hour to accomplish that you might want to consider some other software.

Q: What about an interface to my financial accounting package – or our time clock system?
A: Payroll software can be limited to processing payrolls and producing payroll forms and reports – or it can include a variety of additional products. If it's important to you to have your software interfaced with existing programs, make sure that any payroll package you're considering can be easily "connected" to your other accounting software.

Q: **What if I need a custom program?**
A: Even if the software handles your usual payroll processing, you may run into a situation where you need something the software doesn't do. So you need to know when you buy a payroll package whether or not the vendor is willing and able to do some customization if necessary and what the general time frame and cost is for program modifications.

Q: **What about training?**
A: Ideally a payroll software package should include (in addition to a good help file) an overview of the system, some simple text-based tutorials, videos showing exactly how the software works and covering all the basic features of the system, and an online forum where users can discuss any problems or questions they have about the software.

Q: **What if I run a payroll and then notice an error?**
A: Payroll software should allow you to back up, correct and re-run a payroll if you find that you've made an error or need to add, change or delete some information.

Q: **What if I need payroll information for a workers' compensation audit or a report of an employee's earnings for a previous year?**
A: Your payroll software should maintain a history of previous payroll data and allow you to generate various payment history reports.

Human Resources

Q: **What does a "human resources system" include?**
A: Human resource management systems usually include:
- Job Openings and Applicant tracking.
- Benefits information.
- Tracking employee vacation, sick leave and personal time accrual.
- Training information.
- Performance, pay rate and promotion history.
- Employee review and reminder reports.
- Employee skills and education information.
- Affirmative action tracking.
- New hire reports.
- Wellness and emergency information reports.
- EEO reports.
- OSHA compliance and workers' compensation reports.

Q: **What is "SHRM"?**
A: The Society for Human Resource Management (SHRM) is the world's largest organization devoted to human resource management. The website at www.shrm.org includes information on employment law and other legal issues, sample job descriptions, guidelines for creating company policy manuals, human resource education and certification training, HR publications and community forums.

Q: **What is included in an HR audit?**
A: Typical areas covered in a Human Resources audit include:
- Recruitment and job applicant selection processes.
- Employee record keeping (especially to insure compliance with federal and state record-keeping regulations).
- Compensation and benefits information.
- Safety procedures and risk management practices.
- Employee training and career development programs and policies.
- Employee relations procedures and history.

Q: **What is "strategic HR management"?**
A: Traditionally human resource departments have been concerning with hiring people with the right skill set for specific jobs and dealing with the core functions associated with managing employees – hiring, employee

pay, benefits, and training, as well as generating all required reports. The idea behind strategic HR management is to determine how best to use the human resources department to contribute to the overall goals of the organization – improving individual performance, increasing profits, and providing the organizational flexibility needed to introduce and support new products and services.

Q: **What is a "SWOT" analysis?**
A: A SWOT (Strengths, Weaknesses, Opportunities and Threats) analysis involves defining an organization's goals and identifying those factors that are favorable or unfavorable to achieving those goals. In terms of Human Resources, strengths may include a compensation plan that's competitive with similar companies in the same industry, well-thought out and implemented workplace safety measures, and low employee turn-over. Weaknesses might include an employee benefit plan that is lacking a number of key features or a sub-standard training program. Opportunities may involve the prospective use of new technologies, while threats might include more restrictive employment laws or possible lawsuits from ex-employees.

Q: **What is normally included in an applicant tracking system?**
A: Applicant tracking systems include features such as:
- Posting job openings to the most popular online job boards.
- Collecting applicant information on a web page describing current job openings.
- Qualifying applicants according to pre-screening criteria.
- Automatic parsing and import of resumes to your company's database system.
- Tracking the progress of each job applicant during the hiring process.
- Sending automatic emails to selected job candidates.
- Ensuring that hiring procedures follow federal and state anti-discrimination rules.

Q: **What considerations go into creating an effective job description?**
A: Effective job descriptions should include:
- Basic information such as job title, responsibilities, necessary skills and experience required.
- Any required degrees, licenses, or certifications.
- Tasks that are compatible – for example you wouldn't ordinarily ask an employee to perform both complex analytical tasks and also work as a part-time salesperson.

- Sufficiently detailed information about the job so applicants have a clear idea of what to expect if hired.
- Enough detail so that the job description can be used as a reference tool when interviewing and evaluating applicants.
- At least some indication of what are the possibilities for advancement.

Q: What are some important points to consider in setting up a recruitment program?
A: Some things to consider in developing a recruiting program:
- Have a plan. Know what sources you're going to rely to locate applicants and know how you intend to process applications, resumes and cover letters.
- Decide how much effort you're going to put into researching an applicant's background on social media such as Facebook, LinkedIn and Twitter.
- Be flexible – the best applicant may not necessarily be the person who fits the job description the closest. {Author's note: the best hire I ever made was a young man with a high school diploma who was working as an orderly in a hospital emergency room – for a position where we were looking for a college degree and at least 3 years of experience in the field].
- Constantly evaluate the effectiveness of any ads placed in newspapers or on the web – and be sure to look inside your organization for qualified individuals.

Q: Why should you continue recruiting even if you have no current job openings?
A: It's always a good idea to have a few people identified and on file that you feel would be a good fit for certain jobs in your organization. Job openings in critical areas can occur suddenly – illness, injury or someone leaving abruptly with little or no notice – all those things can make it important to be able to find a qualified replacement in a hurry.

Q: What goes into a policy manual?
A: A company policy manual should cover items such as:
- Recruitment and employment policies
- Employee record keeping
- Employee benefits
- Payroll
- Workplace guidelines
- Employee conduct

Q: **What type of information goes into benefits reporting?**
A: A benefits management system maintains data on the various benefits offered by your company (such as health insurance, 401(k) plans and group term life insurance) and tracks employee eligibility, enrollment and withdrawal dates, along with employee and employer contributions and other pertinent information such as investment options, beneficiaries, and dependents.

Q: **Where can I find information and advice about employee benefit programs?**
A: One good source of benefit facts and figures is the Employee Benefit Research Institute (www.ebri.org). You can find FAQs about benefits, special reports, news briefs, and a variety of other information on benefits at the EBRI website.

Q: **What features are included in employee time off accrual reporting?**
A: Employee accrual systems usually keep track of sick days, vacation days and personal days accrued, used, and scheduled. An accrual system may also calculate days earned based on how long an employee has worked for the company, his or her seniority level and other factors.

Q: **What type of training information should a company keep?**
A: Most companies have training sessions for new employees, "continuing education" type training and/or training to familiarize employees with new equipment or new procedures. Information to keep on file might include: title, date, location, cost, instructor name, attendees and number of hours for each training session. If the training involves multiple sessions the data may also include the scheduled training dates and which sessions each employee has attended.

Q: **What type of items go into an employee review?**
A: Performance reviews can take different forms (text-based, numerical, comparison-based) but they generally include evaluations such as:
- Skill and proficiency in carrying out job assignments
- Ability to plan and organize workload
- Assumes accountability for assigned responsibilities
- Communicates effectively with peers and supervisors
- Capable of working independently or in groups
- Willing to take on additional responsibilities
- Delegates responsibility when appropriate
- Manages subordinates effectively and fairly
- Shows proficiency at improving work methods and procedures

Q: **What about "exit interviews"?**
A: It's a good idea to conduct exit interviews with employees who are leaving – it's an opportunity to get their viewpoint on everything from your company's work environment to your training and supervisors. Typical questions that could be asked during an exit interview include:

- Why are you leaving?
- What do think of working conditions here?
- Do you think you were adequately trained?
- How would you rate your supervisor(s)?
- Do you think the pay rate was fair?
- What do think about the employee benefits?
- Are there other benefits that you feel should be provided?
- Do you feel there was an adequate chance for advancement?
- How would you rate the general morale here?
- What did you like the most and the least about your job?

Q: **In HR terms, what is a "data warehouse"?**
A: A data warehouse is a large database of employee information, particularly "employee metrics" - measurements that attempt to quantify each employee's productivity, efficiency, and other items that contribute to the employee's overall "performance" rating.

Q: **What is Form I-9?**
A: Form I-9 is a U.S. Citizenship and Immigration Services form used by an employer to verify a new employee's identity and eligibility to be hired for employment in the United States. The job applicant must produce documents establishing his or her identity and employment authorization. Employers must keep the completed I-9 on file for three years from the start date of employment or for one year following the employee's termination, whichever is later.

Q: **How soon after hiring does a company have to complete a Form I-9 for the new employee?**
A: A form I-9 (Employment Eligibility Form) must be completed within 72 hours after the individual is hired.

Q: **What document is considered to be the definitive guideline covering the legality of employee selection procedures?**
A: The UGESP (Uniform Guidelines on Employee Selection Procedures).

Q: **When dealing with human resources, what are "protected groups"?**

A: "Protected groups" are those whose members are covered by federal or state anti-discrimination laws. The protected categories are: race, color, religion, age, sex, national origin, and disability handicaps.

Q: **What is "adverse impact" in regards to human resources?**
A: Adverse impact (also referred to as "disparate impact") refers to employment practices that have a discriminatory effect on a protected group, even if the effect is unintentional. Statistically, adverse impact occurs if the rate of selection of new employees from a protected class is less than 80% of the rate for the class with the highest selection rate. At that point the employer should either adjust hiring procedures or compile proof of the procedures as a business necessity.

Q: **What are EAPs?**
A: Employee Assistance Programs (EAPs) originated in the 1970s as a way to provide assistance for employees with various types of personal problems and are often handled by the HR department. Areas in which EAP providers can assist employees include:
- Alcohol and substance abuse.
- Legal aid sources for employees with legal problems.
- Marriage counseling.
- Financial counseling.
- Mental health evaluation and referral.
- Preretirement planning.

Q: **Is seniority a factor in determining equal pay for men and women under the Equal Pay Act of 1963?**
A: No. For men and women working at essentially the same job, skill and effort are factors in determining pay level, but not seniority.

Q: **If an employee, Tom Jones, is out on leave under the FMLA (Family Medical Leave Act) when bonuses are paid to all full-time employees, is the employer required to pay Tom's bonus when he returns to work?**
A: Yes – under the FMLA employees out on leave are to be treated the same as all currently working employees.

Q: **What is the "fellow servant rule"?**
A: Under the "fellow servant" rule, an employee who is injured because of the actions of a co-worker cannot bring a personal injury action against his or her employer. The fellow servant rule doesn't apply to cases involving workers' compensation – the injured employee can recover workers' compensation benefits even if the injury was caused by a co-worker.

Q: **What is the EEOC?**
A: The Equal Employment Opportunity Commission (EEOC) is the federal agency that enforces federal anti-discrimination laws in regard to employment practices.

Q: **What happens if someone files a complaint with the EEOC charging you with unfair employment practices?**
A: In general, these are the steps in an EEOC investigation:
1) The EEOC will notify you that a complaint has been filed and will supply you with a copy of the charges.
2) You can accept mediation and an EEOC member will meet with someone from your company and the person filing the complaint to try to resolve the issue.
3) If you refuse mediation or mediation doesn't resolve the issue the EEOC will conduct an investigation which generally involves interviews with members of your company and a review of any pertinent company documents.
4) Once the investigation is completed the EEOC will render a decision. If the EEOC finds against the person filing the complaint it will also issue that individual a "right-to-sue" notice. If the EEOC finds valid grounds for the complaint it will attempt to get you to participate in a concilliation process. If you refuse concilliation or concilliation fails the EEOC will either take you to court or issue a "right-to-sue" notice to the complaintant.

Q: **What is an EEO-1 report and who has to file it?**
A: The EEO-1 report is a report of an organization's employees categorized by race/ethnicity, gender and job category. Most companies with over 100 employees are required to file an EEO-1 report annually. The employment data on the report has to taken from one pay period in July, August or September of the current year and the filing deadline is September 30th. Multi-location companies are required to file a report for the headquarters location and for each of the other physical business locations (even for those with less than 50 employees).

Q: **How should I submit my EEO-1 report?**
A: The preferred method of submitting EEO-1 reports is through the EEO-1 Online Filing Application or as an electronically transmitted ASCII text file. EEO-1 reports can also be submitted as computer printouts. Specifications for creating an EEO-1 data file as available at:
        http://www.eeoc.gov/eeo1survey

Q: **Which businesses have to keep records for OSHA (Occupational Safety and Health Administration)?**
A: Businesses in certain industries with more than 10 employees are required to display OSHA safety and health information (OSHA 3165 or state equivalent) in their workplace and to record any occupational injuries or illnesses as they occur using OSHA form 300, Log of Work-Related Injuries and Illnesses. However, OSHA record-keeping is not required for most employers in retail trade, finance, insurance, real estate, and service industries.

Q: **If a business has to keep OSHA records, is that business subject to inspection?**
A: Yes, every business covered by the OSH Act has to comply with federal and state safety standards and is subject to inspection by federal or state officials.

Q: **Who should I contact to find out if a substance we're using in a manufacturing or other process is toxic?**
A: Contact NIOSH, the National Institute for Occupational Safety and Health (http://www.cdc.gov/niosh/).

Q: **What is OFCCP compliance?**
A: Contractors and sub-contractors working on federal government contracts worth over ten thousand dollars are required to comply with OFCCP (Office of Federal Contract Compliance Programs) regulations. Basically OFCCP compliance means you as an employer have to abide by basic affirmative action and equal opportunity (EEO) requirements that have to do with eliminating discrimination in hiring due to gender, race or ethnicity of applicants.

Q: **What is the "Portal-to-Portal Act"?**
A: The Portal-to-Portal Act of 1947 defines what employee non-work activities are subject to minimum wage and overtime rules. Generally speaking, acitivities that are outside of normal working hours and are not controlled by the employer (such as travel to and from the work site or arriving for work early and waiting for the start of the workday) are not subject to minimum wage or overtime regulations unless covered by a contract or by custom. Activities during the workday (such as coffee breaks or fire drills) normally are subject to wage and hour laws.

Q: **What is the main requirement of the Employee Retirement Income Security Act?**
A: ERISA makes it mandatory for the administrator of an employee benefit plan to furnish participating employees and beneficiaries with a

summary plan description (SPD) describing the participants benefits, rights and responsibilities under the plan.

Q: **Is my company subject to Title VII of the Civil Rights Act of 1964?**
A: Title VII of the Civil Rights Act of 1964 prevents discrimination in employment because of race, color, religion or national origin. It applies to all employers with 15 or more employees.

Q: **Which federal agency enforces Affirmative Action?**
A: The Office of Federal Contract Compliance (OFCCP).

Q: **Can an employee be fired on the basis that he or she has been garnished for a single debt?**
A: The Consumer Credit Protection Act prevents an employee from being terminated solely due to the fact that his or her wages are being garnished for one debt.

Q: **What is OSHA?**
A: The Occupational Health and Safety Administration is the federal agency charged with issuing workplace health and safety regulations. OSHA conducts various training, compliance assistance and health and safety recognition programs.

Q: **What is the "Employee Right-to-Know law"?**
A: The Employee Right-to-Know law is an OSHA (Occupational Health and Safety Administration) standard that requires organizations handling hazardous materials to inform all employees about any chemical hazards to which they may be exposed.

Q: **If an employee requires first aid treatment does that incident have to be reported to OSHA?**
A: Generally minor injuries requiring first aid do not have to be reported to the Occupational Health and Safety Administration.

Q: **How quickly does OSHA Form 301 (injury and illness report) have to be submitted once the employer learns of a work-related injury?**
A: Form 301 has to be submitted to OSHA within 7 days.

Q: **If a union loses a representation election how quickly can they call another election?**
A: The union has to wait at least 12 months before they can call another election.

Q: **Where can I get more information about Human Resource Management?**
A: Workforce (www.workforce.com) offers newsletters, blogs, forums and articles on a wide variety of topics including employee compensation, benefits, HR administration, workplace safety, motivating employees, employee training and skills development, applicant interviewing and HR trends.

Federal Laws That Affect Payroll

Q: **What is the FLSA?**
A: The Federal Labor Standards Act of 1938 (usually referred to as the Federal Wage and Hour Law) covers federal minimum wage requirements, child labor, wage garnishments, and overtime pay requirements. There have been a number of amendments to the Act over the years, most of them dealing with increases in the federal minimum wage. Other amendments include the Equal Pay Act of 1963 (making it illegal to pay workers lower wages based strictly on their sex) and the Age Discrimination in Employment Act (ADEA) of 1967 (prohibiting discrimination based strictly on age). The FLSA **does not** require employers to pay extra wages for work on weekends or holidays, provide vacation or severance pay, or grant employees vacation time.

Q: **Are there employees who are exempt from the FLSA?**
A: There are a number of categories of employees who are exempt from the provisions of the FLSA including:

- Executives (must be paid a salary of at least $455 per week, must customarily and regularly direct the work of 2 or more other employees, must have the authority to hire and fire, and their primary duty must be managing the company or a sub-division of the company).
- Administrators (must be paid a salary of at least $455 per week and their primary duty must be office or non-manual work directly related to the management of the business).
- Professionals (must be paid a salary of at least $455 per week and their primary duties must be work requiring advanced knowledge for learned professionals or work requiring imagination or talent for creative professionals).
- Computer Employees (must be paid a salary of at least $455 per week, and must be a systems analyst, programmer, computer engineer, or someone holding a similar position).
- Outside Salespeople (primary duty must be sales and must be customarily and regularly working away from the employer's place or places of business).
- Agricultural workers.
- Police officers and firefighters.
- Hospital and nursing home workers.

Note: Exempt employees normally have to be paid on a salary basis – however administrative, professional and computer employees can also be paid on a "fee basis" (paid by job) as long as the time spent on the job and the fee work out to at least $455 per week.

In addition there are certain employees who are exempt from just the overtime pay provisions of the FLSA, including:

- Employees covered by a collective bargaining agreement.
- Farm workers.
- Railroad and air carrier employees.
- Taxi drivers.
- Seamen on American vessels.

Q: **Does the FLSA require employers to pay holiday pay?**
A: FLSA regulations don't require employers to pay vacation, sick or holiday pay.

Q: **Do FLSA overtime rules apply to non-exempt employees time spent traveling to or from their place of work?**
A: FLSA overtime regulations don't apply to time spent traveling to and from work unless there is a contract or an established custom to the contrary. In additional employers aren't required to pay for time spent in activities before or after the normal work day unless those activities are essential to performing the employee's job.

Q: **Can I dock an employee's salary who is exempt from the FLSA?**
A: Normally, no. However you can dock an exempt employee's salary in certain cases:

- Full day absences under a sick or disability plan or for personal reasons.
- Unpaid leave under the Family and Medical Leave Act (FMLA).
- Disciplinary suspensions for one or more full days.
- Major safety violations.
- Weeks where the employee doesn't perform any work during the week.
- To offset money the employee receives for military or jury duty.

Q: **What is the Federal Insurance Contributions Act?**
A: The Federal Insurance Contributions Act (FICA) instituted a mandatory payroll tax on both employees and employers to fund Social Security and Medicare, the federal programs that provide benefits for retirees, disabled workers, and children of deceased workers. Social Security cover old-age, survivors and disability insurance (OASDI), while Medicare provides hospital insurance benefits.

Q: **What is the "small business health care credit"?**
A: The Patient Protection and Affordable Health Care Act of 2010

includes tax credits for small businesses that provide health care coverage to their employees. For tax years 2010 through 2013, the maximum credit was 35 percent for small business employers and 25 percent for small tax-exempt employers. In 2014 employers are eligible for up to a 50% credit of premiums (35% for tax exempt organizations). The tax credit can be carried back or forward to other tax years and, in addition, eligible businesses can also claim an expense deduction for the health insurance premiums in excess of the credit. To be eligible for the tax credit a business must cover at least 50 percent of the cost of single (not family) health care coverage for each employee, must have fewer than 25 full time equivalent employees (FTEs), and those employees must have average wages of less than $50,000 a year. Also, the amount of the credit works on a sliding scale; the smaller the business or charity, the larger the credit. For the full 50% credit, a business must have 10 or fewer FTEs who are paid less than $25,000 on average. You can use Form 8941 (www.irs.gov) to calculate the tax credit and you can also use the tax credit calculator at:
 http://www.nfib.com/issues-elections/healthcare/credit-calculator
to estimate your credit. "C" Corporations can use Form 8941 to report the credit; partnerships and S corporations report the credit on Schedule K and pass it through to the shareholders or partners. For more information go to:
http://www.irs.gov/newsroom/article/0,,id=223666,00.html

Q: **What are some other federal laws that affect employers?**
A: Federal laws that employers should know about include:
- Title VII of the Civil Rights Act of 1964 - provides for fair employment practices and forbids employers to discriminate in hiring, firing, promoting, or compensating employees based on race, religion, gender or nationality. The act covers all employers who are involved in an industry "affecting commerce" and who employ 15 or more workers for each business day in each of 20 or more weeks in the current or preceding calendar year. Guidelines for enforcement of Title VII are established by the Equal Employment Opportunity Commission (EEOC).
- Immigration Reform and Control Act of 1986 - makes it illegal for employers to hire aliens who aren't authorized to work in the United States and requires employers to verify an individual's employment eligibility by examining certain documents and having the prospective employee fill out a Form I-9 (Employment Eligibility Verification).
- Federal Personal Responsibility and Work Opportunity Reconciliation Act of 1996 - PRWORA requires each state to establish a new-hire reporting program. Employers must report

the name, address, and social security number of every new employee within 20 days of the hire date to the appropriate state agency. The state forwards the information to the federal Office of Child Support Enforcement (OCSE) to be entered into a national directory to help enforce child support obligations.

- Employee Retirement Income Security Act of 1974 - ERISA covers employee pension plans set up or maintained by any employer or employee organization and regulates how pension funds are gathered and disbursed, who controls them and how to handle various situations that may arise. ERISA was established primarily to make sure workers who contribute to a pension fund over the years receive benefits from those funds in accordance with their years of service. If an employer maintains a pension plan, ERISA specifies when employees must be allowed to become participants, how long they have to work before they have a non-forfeitable interest in their pension, how long participants can be away from their job before it affects their benefits, and whether their spouses have a right to a part of their pension in the event of their death.
- Age Discrimination in Employment Act (ADEA) of 1967 – This act prohibits employers, employment agencies and labor unions from discriminating on the basis of age in their employment practices and covers all employers with 20 or more workers. Employers subject to ADEA rules should keep a file of all employment applications (with notations as to their disposition) and all records relating to promotions, terminations, merit programs, incentive payment plans, etc.
- Americans with Disabilities Act – The 1990 Americans with Disabilities Act (ADA) prohibits employers with 15 or more employees, employment agencies and labor organizations from discriminating against qualified job applicants on the basis of their disability. In addition, accommodations such as wheelchair-accessible restrooms and ramps have to be provided for handicapped workers.
- Family and Medical Leave Act of 1993 – The Family and Medical Leave Act (FMLA) requires employers with 50 or more employees within a 75-mile radius for at least 20 weeks in the current or preceding calendar year to provide workers unpaid leave for a family or medical emergency. Employers must offer workers up to 12 weeks of unpaid leave in cases of childbirth, adoption, or serious illness or injury to the employee, the employee's children, spouse, parent or a family member on active military duty. The leave can be taken all at once or spaced out in separate weeks, days or hours, although the entire

amount of leave has to be taken within 12 months of the family or medical emergency. The employer must continue health coverage for the employee while the employee is on leave and must guarantee that the employee will return to the same job or an equivalent job. Employers can exempt the highest-paid ten percent of their workforce, as well as employees who haven't worked for them for at least one year or at least 1,250 hours in the past 12 months. Note: Some states (like New Jersey) have established *paid* family leave plans, funded by payroll deductions.

The Affordable Care Act (Obamacare)

The Patient Protection and Affordable Care Act (also referred to as the "ACA" or "Obamacare" means big changes for employers and employees. The major provisions of the bill went into effect on January 1, 2015.

So, what does an employer need to know about complying with the law?

The health care bill requires nearly all Americans to obtain health insurance. The law expects that most workers will get that coverage through their employers and has created a system of subsidies and penalties to make this possible. If you're an employer, the size of your workforce is important, as the law has different requirements depending on the number of employees you have.

Here are the major aspects of the health care bill as it relates to employers:

Q: **Which businesses does the law affect?**
A: The ACA doesn't impose a straight-forward requirement that employers offer health insurance to workers but it does impose penalties on certain categories of employers who fail to do so.

Q: **What is a "small business"?**
A: Under the Act, a small business is not specifically defined, but a number of sections of the law apply only to organizations with fewer than 25 employees (for more detail see below.) However, under some sections of the law, the effective company size is 50 or 100 employees.

Q: **How does the Affordable Care Act determine the number of employees an organization employs?**
A: Determining then number of employees involves counting both full-time and part-time employees. An employer is required to count the number of regular full-time employees (those that work a minimum of 30 hours per week on the average) plus any "full-time equivalent" employees or "FTEs". To calculate the number of FTEs in a given month the employer must add up the hours (up to 120 hours per employee) of all part-time workers (those who worked an average of less than 30 hours per week) and divide by 120 hours. The result (rounded down) is the number of equivalent full-time employees. For example a company who has 9 full-time employees plus 5 part-time employees who worked a total of 380 hours during the month would have the equivalent of 12 full-

time employees (9 plus 380 divided by 120).

For salaried employees who are not paid by the hour there are 3 options for determining hours worked:

- The same method used for hourly employees (requires calculating hours worked for each salaried person during the pay period).
- A "days-worked" equivalency method (each salaried employee is credited with 8 hours for each day worked).
- A "weeks-worked" equivalency method (each salaried employee is credited with 40 hours for each week worked).

Although part-time employees count toward the 50 employee limit in determining "large" employers, employers are not required to offer health insurance to part-time employees. Because an employer may not be sure how many hours a particular employee (such as a seasonal worker) my work during a calendar year, the ACA allows the employer to wait up to 12 months to retroactively determine the status of variable-hour employees. The employer has to choose a "measurement period" of between 3 and 12 months to calculate whether 30 or more hours per week are worked by that person and whether the employee is entitled to coverage for a certain period thereafter.

Q: What are "insurance exchanges"?

A: Beginning January 1, 2014, health insurance will be available to individuals and small businesses through state-run "exchanges." These will require insurance companies to compete for business in the marketplace. The objective is to make it it easier for individuals and small businesses to obtain health insurance at a lower price. The exchange program for small businesses, known as the Small Business Health Options Program (SHOP), will allow small businesses to pool together to increase their purchasing power. This will allow these businesses to offer health insurance to their employees at rates similar to those available to large corporations.

SHOP is available to small businesses with up to 100 employees, although states have the option to limit participation to businesses with 50 employees or less until 2016. If a business participating in SHOP grows to over 100 employees, it may continue to take advantage of the program. Beginning in 2017, states may choose to allow businesses with more than 100 employees to participate in SHOP as well.

The exchange program is also important because larger employers may be penalized if some of their employees choose to obtain insurance through an exchange and not through the company's insurance plan (for more detail see below.)

Q: Are employers required to provide health insurance to their employees?

A: Businesses with fewer than 50 employees are exempt from having to provide health insurance. However, as explained above, such smaller employers may choose to offer health insurance at a reasonable cost by participating in a SHOP exchange.

Larger businesses are subject to a number of requirements and potential penalties, depending on the number of employees they have and the type of coverage they provide:

- Companies with 50 or more full-time or full-time equivalent employees will be required to offer health insurance to their workers and the workers' dependent children beginning in 2015 (however coverage for workers' spouses will not be mandatory).

- Automatic enrollment: Employers with more than 200 employees are required to enroll new employees in their health care plan, subject to any normal waiting period. Employers must also provide notice of employees' right to opt out of automatic enrollment.

- Notice of coverage options: Employers must give employees notice about the availability of an insurance exchange..

- Beginning in 2015 employers are required to keep track of the full or part-time status of each employee and report that status to the IRS.

Q: What about new employers?
A: A new employer - an employer not in existence during the entire preceding year - may be considered a large employers if it is reasonably expected to employ at least 50 full-time employees (taking into account FTEs) on business days during the current calendar year and it actually employes 50 full-time employees during the calendar year.

Q: What is the "shared responsibility" (or "play or pay") portion of the ACA?
A: Large business (over 50 employees) come under the Employer Shared Responsibility Provisions of the ACA. These provisions include:

- A penalty for not providing insurance: Employers with over 50 employees that do not provide insurance must pay a penalty of $2,000 for every employee in the company if even one employee chooses to obtain insurance through an exchange. However, the first 30 employees are not counted in calculation of the penalty. Example: an employer with 75 employees would pay the penalty for 45 workers, or $90,000 (45 x $2.000).

- A penalty for providing insurance that isn't "affordable" or doesn't provide "minimum value". Coverage is considered affordable if an employee's required contribution toward the employer's lowest cost self-only coverage doesn't exceed 9.5 percent of his or her household income. Under the ACA an insurance plan fails to provide minimum value if the plan's share of the total cost of benefits provided under the plan is less than 60% of those costs. If the employer's plan fails to provide minimum value, employees may be eligible to receive a premium tax credit. Employers with more than 50 employees that do provide insurance must pay a penalty if any of their employees receive a premium tax credit to help pay for insurance. The penalty equals $3,000 per worker who uses the subsidy OR $750 for every employee at the company, whichever is less.

Note: The IRS is expected to provide a minimum value calculator which will allow an employer to enter information such as deductibles and co-pays in order to determine if their plan meets the minimum value requirement.

Q: What information do employers have to share with their employees?
A: Under the ACA employers with 50 or more full-time or full-time equivalent employees must:
- Provide written notice informing their employees about their state's insurance Exchange, including instructions as how to contact the Exchange.
- Notify employees if the plan offered by the employer doesn't meet the "minimum value" standard and must let employees know that they may be eligible for a premium tax credit and a cost-sharing reduction if they purchase a health care plan through the state's insurance Exchange.
- Notify employees that if they purchase a plan through the state's insurance Exchange, they may lose the employer's contribution to health benefits.

Q: Is there help for small businesses to provide insurance for their workers?
A: From 2010 through 2013, businesses which had fewer than 25 employees and paid average annual wages of $50,000 or less were eligible for a tax credit of up to 35% if they paid for at least 50% of their employees' health insurance costs.

Beginning in 2014, small businesses that purchase health insurance for their employees through SHOP can receive a two-year small business tax credit of up to 50% of the cost of the premiums. Employers with 10 or fewer employees with an annual average wage of $25,000 or less are eligible for the full tax credit. Note: The employee average annual wage limit of $50,000 will be indexed by the cost of living.

While small businesses are not required to obtain insurance for their employees through the exchanges, the available tax credits may spur many smaller employers to purchase coverage for their workforce.

Note: Business owners, partners and family members of small business owners do not generally count as employees for purposes of qualifying for the tax credit.

Q: Will there be special taxes to help pay for the Affordable Care Act?
A: Beginning in 2013 an additional 0.9% Medicare tax was applied to any employee whose FICA taxable earnings exceeds $200,000 for the calendar year. The additional 0.9% (making the total Medicare percentage 1.45% + 0.9% = 2.35%) will apply only to the wages in excess of $200,000. (Note: employers do not have to pay a matching amount for the additional Medicare tax).

Q: Where can I find additional information about the Affordable Care Act?
A: Here are two websites that may be helpful:

- http://www.sba.gov/healthcare
- www.irs.gov/uac (go to this URL and enter "affordable care act" in the search box on the upper right)

ACA Affordability and Minimum Value Calculations

Q: **What is "minimum value health insurance" under the ACA?**
A: Coverage meets minimum value standards if the plan pays at least 60% of the actuarial value of benefits covered under the plan.

Q: **What is the "actuarial value" of an insurance plan?**
A: The percentage of total average costs for covered benefits that a plan will cover. For example, if a plan has an actuarial value of 60%, the plan would cover 60% of the cost of all covered benefits and the employee would be responsible for the other 40% of the cost.

Q: **What is considered "affordable insurance" under the ACA?**
A: Coverage is considered "affordable" if no full-time employee is required to pay more than 9.5% of his or her "household income" for self-only coverage under the employer's lowest-cost option that provides minimum value.

Q: **How does an employer calculate affordability?**
There are three methods (or "safe harbors") for calculating the affordability of the health insurance offered to employees. They are:
- W-2 income. As long as no employee is paying more than 9.5% of his or her W-2 Box 1 wages, the coverage is "affordable". For employees who are not full time for an entire calendar year the Box 1 wages must be multiplied by a fraction (the number of months during which coverage was offered divided by the number of months the individual was employed during the calendar year). Also, for employees that have pre-tax deductions such as cafeteria or 401(k) plans, the Box 1 wages will be understated by those amounts which could mean the employer's "affordable" coverage is less than it really needs to be.
- Rate of pay. To calculate "affordability" under this method, multiply 9.5% times the hourly rate of pay for the lowest paid hourly employee (as of the beginning of the plan year) times 130 hours. However, an employer can't use this method if any employee's wages are cut during the year. Also, an employer can only multiply by 130 hours regardless of how many hours the employee actually works per month.
- Federal poverty line. To determine affordability with this method make sure the employees' premiums are not more than 100 percent of the individual FPL ($11,670 for 2014/15) times 9.5%.

This "safe harbor" is essentially fail-safe, although the employer may end up paying more per employee than with the other methods.

Q: Does an employer have to use one of the three safe harbors listed above?
A: No, an employer can apply a different method if the method is applied in a uniform and consistent basis for all employees in a particular category.

Affordable Care Act Reporting

Q: **What reports will employers have to file under the ACA?**
A: There are two forms for employers to file, Form 1095-B (and the transmittal form 1094-B) and Form 1095-C (and its transmittal form 1094-C). Which form an employer has to file depends on the employer's health plan and number of employees. Note: If an employer has less than 50 employees and does not offer an insurance plan there is no reporting requirement.

Q: **Which employers have to file Form 1095-B or Form 1095-C?**
A: For employers with less than 50 employees who sponsor a health insurance plan through an insurance company, there is no filing requirement – the insurer will file the From 1095-Bs for the employer. However, employers with fewer than 50 employees who are self-insured must file Form 1094-B and the accompanying 1095-B forms for any employees covered under their insurance plan. Large employers (50 or more employees) and small employers (less than 50 employees) who are part of a group of companies that combined have more than 50 employees are treated as follows:
- Employers in this category who do not offer health insurance must file Form 1094-C and the accompanying 1095-C forms.
- Employers in this category who sponsor an insurance plan through an insurance company must file Form 1094-C and the accompanying 1095-C forms for all full-time employees – however the insurance carrier will file Form 1094-B and the 1095-B forms.
- Employers in this category who are self-insured have to file Form 1094-C and 1095-C including Part III but do not have to file 1094-B or 1095-B.

Q: **What are IRS Forms 1094-C and 1095-C?**
A: As part of the ACA (Affordable Care Act) the IRS has to identify which Applicable Large Employers offered health insurance (and the right kind of insurance) to full-time employees during the year in order to assess penalties for employers who don't comply with the ACA. To accomplish that goal, the IRS is requiring all Applicable Large Employers to fill out a Form 1095-C for any worker who was a full-time employee for one or more months in 2016. The 1095-C forms (like W-2 forms) must be supplied to employees and sent to the IRS by March 31st, 2017. The 1095-C forms sent to the IRS also have to be accompanied by a

transmittal form, Form 1094-C (similar to Form W-3 which accompanies W-2 forms).

Q: **Who has to file 1095-C forms?**
A: Every Applicable Large Employer must file a 1095-C form for each worker who was a full-time employee for at least one month during the preceding calendar year.

Q: **Who is an "Applicable Large Employer"?**
A: An applicable large employer (ALE) is an employer who averages at least 50 full-time employees (including full-time equivalent employees) for the calendar year.

Q: **So, if I average less than 50 full-time employees for the year I'm not an ALE?**
A: It depends. Organizations that are under common ownership or control are combined in order to determine if they have 50 or more full-time employees. If you have 30 full-time employees and you have a sister company with 25 full-time employees, then you are considered an Applicable Large Employer Member and are required to file 1095-C forms for your company.

Q: **What is a "full-time employee"?**
A: Under the ACA, a full-time employee is an employee who averages at least 30 service hours a week or 130 hours a month.

Q: **What is a "full-time equivalent employee"?**
A: Full-time equivalent employees are determined by adding up the hours of your part-time employees (individuals who averaged less than 30 hours a week) and dividing that total by the number of part-time employees.

Q: **How do I determine how many full-time employees I have during a given month? And how many full-time employees do I have on the average for the year?**
A: Combine the hours of all part-time employees for a given month (up to 120 hours per employee) and divide the total by 120. Then add that total to the number of full-time employees (individuals who averaged 30 hours or more a week) to get the number of full-time and full-time equivalent employees for the month. To determine your average number of full-time employees for the year, add together the number of full-time and full-time equivalent employees for each month of the calendar year and divide by 12.

Q: Is there a specific method or time period that should be used to identify full-time employees for coverage purposes?
A: The ACA specifies two methods for identifying full-time employees. The standard method for identifying full-time employees is the "look-back measurement method". The look-back method involves 3 different periods:
- A "measurement period" for counting hours of service (also called a "standard measurement period" or an "initial measurement period"). The standard measurement period (which deals with ongoing employees) must be between 6 and 12 months in length.
- A "stability period" during which the employee is treated either as full-time or non-full-time for Plan eligibility purposes. The stability period must be at least 6 months and must be at least as long as the SMP (standard measurement period).
- An "administrative period" between the SMP and the stability period which allows for Plan enrollment and dis-enrollment and can last for up to 90 days.

Q: Are there any employees whose hours I don't have to include?
A: Yes – leased employees, employees working outside the United States, certain seasonal employees, sole proprietors, partners, 2-percent S corporation shareholders, certain sales people, and workers described in IRS regulations as real estate agents.

Q: Do I have to count employees who are eligible for other forms of health insurance, such as Medicare, Medicaid, or insurance through a spouse's employer?
A: Yes, outside of the exceptions noted above, all employees are counted.

Q: If an employee was full-time for one month but left before our normal 60 day waiting period before offering insurance was over, do we still have to provide a 1095-C form for that individual?
A: Yes, any employee who was considered full-time for at least one month during the year must receive a 1095-C form, regardless of whether or not coverage was offered.

Q: Can you give me an example of how to determine my ALE status if I have 40 full-time employees for each month in 2016 and 15 part-time employees each month, each of whom works 60 hours per month?
A: The combined monthly hours for your part-time employees is 60 hours x 15 or 900 hours. Divide that total by 120 (the maximum number of

hours per part-time worker per month) and you get 7.5. The number 7.5 represents the number of "full-time equivalent employees" per month. Multiply 7.5 by 12 months and add the number of full-time workers (40) times 12 months. That total comes to 90 + 480 or 570 for the year. Then divide 570 by 12 months, which gives you an average of 47.5 "full-time" employees per month - which, under ACA rules, is rounded down to 47, the nearest whole number. In this case even though you have 55 employees you only have an average of 47 full-time and full-time equivalent employees per month so you are not an Applicable Large Employer.

Q: **My company has 55 full-time employees in 2016 (no part-time employees) but I don't offer health insurance – will I be subject to penalties?**
A: If you don't offer coverage, you will owe a penalty if any full time employee is eligible for and purchases subsidized coverage through a Marketplace exchange.

Q: **My company is not an ALE or member of an ALE group – do I have to provide health insurance to my employees? Can I be penalized for not providing insurance or for providing insurance that doesn't meet the standards of the ACA?**
A: No to both questions.

Q: **My company is self-insured but it's not an ALE – do I have to file any forms?**
A: Yes. You must file Form 1094-B (transmittal form) and a Form 1095-B for each employee.

Q: **If my company is not self-insured and is not an ALE, then I don't have to file any ACA forms?**
A: Correct.

Q: **What is a "QHP"?**
A: A Qualified Health Plan or "QHP" is one that is certified by the Health Insurance Marketplace, provides essential health benefits, follows established limits on cost-sharing (like deductibles, co-payments, and out-of-pocket maximum amounts), and meets other requirements.

Q: **What is a Minimum Essential Coverage (MEC) health insurance plan?**
A: An MEC plan is a more limited version of a QHP.

Q: **What is "Minimum Value"?**

A: Under the ACA a health insurance plan is considered to provide "minimum value" if it covers 60% of the total allowed cost of benefits that are expected to be incurred under the plan. Employers can use a minimum value calculator developed by HHS (the Department of Human Health Services) to determine if their insurance plan provides minimum value.

Q: What health coverage is considered "affordable coverage" by the ACA?
A: The ACA considers health insurance to be affordable if it meets any one of three IRS "safe harbors" - that is, if the employee's required premium co-share of the lowest cost, self-only coverage:
Is not greater than 9.5% of the employee's W-2 Box 1 taxable income
Is not greater than 9.5% of the employee's rate of pay on the first day of the coverage period (usually the first day of the plan period)
Is not greater than 9.5% of the current year's US mainland Federal Poverty Level (FPL) for a single individual.

Q: So what exactly can I be penalized for if I'm an Applicable Large Employer?
A: You can be subject to penalties for several reasons under Section 4980H(a) and Section 4980H(b) of the ACA:
1) Failing to offer health coverage or offering health coverage to less than 95% of your full-time employees and their dependents - and at least one of the full-time employees receives a premium tax credit to help pay for coverage obtained on the Marketplace.
2) You offer health coverage to at least 95% of your full-time employees, but at least one full-time employee obtains a premium tax credit to help pay for coverage on a Marketplace because the coverage you offered was either unaffordable to the employee or it didn't provide minimum value.

Q: Can I be penalized for not providing coverage if an employee is terminated during the month when coverage would have been offered if the person had remained employed?
A: No, in that case the employee is treated as having been offered coverage during that month.

Q: I'm an ALE. If I offer affordable health care coverage that provides minimum value to my full-time employees and offer health coverage to their dependents, can I be subject to Employer Shared Responsibility penalties if some of my employees buy health insurance through a Marketplace?
A: No.

Q: **What if the insurance I offer isn't affordable and one of my full-time employees purchases health insurance through a Marketplace – am I subject to a penalty?**
A: Not unless the employee who bought insurance from the Marketplace receives a premium tax credit.

Q: **Who does the ACA consider a dependent?**
A: The ACA defines a dependent as a "child" of the employee who hasn't reached age 26 (excluding foster children, stepchildren, and most children who aren't U.S. Citizens or nationals). Note: ACA regulations state that a child is a dependent for the full month in which he or she turns age 26.

Q: **Do the ACA Employer Shared Responsibility provisions only apply to applicable large employers that have for-profit businesses?**
A: No. All applicable large employers are subject to the ACA provisions, including for-profit, non-profit and government entity employers.

Q: **Are there periods of time when I'm not responsible for offering coverage to an employee?**
A: Yes, there are a number of "limited non-assessment periods" when an ALE (Applicable Large Employer) isn't required to offer health coverage to an employee:

- If an employer is in the first year as an applicable large employer, coverage doesn't have to be offered until April 1 of that year.
- Coverage doesn't have to be offered to a new worker (who is expected to be a full-time employee) for the first 3 months of employment if the employee is otherwise eligible for coverage under the employer's group health plan.
- If a variable-hour or seasonal employee changes status during his or her initial measurement period such that he or she can now be reasonably assumed to be a full-time employee, the employer has 3 calendar months from the date of change of status to provide coverage.

Affordable Care Act – Form 1094-C

Q: **What is Form 1094-C?**
A: As mentioned in the overview, 1094-C is the transmittal form that accompanies the 1095-C forms submitted to the IRS (similar to Form W-3, the transmittal form that accompanies W-2 forms submitted to the Social Security Administration).

Q: **In Part I, line 2 asks for my FEIN/EIN – can I use my Social Security number if I don't have an EIN?**
A: No, you must have a Federal Employer's Identification Number in order to file a 1094-C (and the accompanying 1095-C forms).

Q: **My company is a member of a controlled group under a parent company – which address should I enter on lines 3 through 6?**
A: You can enter your company's address or the parent company's address – just be sure that the address you use on the 1094-C is the same address you use on the 1095-C forms.

Q: **What do I enter on lines 9 through 16?**
A: Unless you're a government employer you can skip lines 9 through 16.

Q: **I understand that I'm supposed to enter the number of accompanying 1095-C forms on line 18, but what does box 19 mean about this being the "authoritative transmittal"?**
A: If you are sending all your 1095-C forms along with this 1094-C, check Box 19 to declare this as your "authoritative" transmittal and complete Parts II, III and IV as applicable. However, for example, if you have already submitted an "authoritative" 1094-C and accompanying 1095-C forms and discover that you left out one or more employees, then you need to fill out a second 1094-C to go with those additional 1095-C forms – and that second 1094-C will not be your "authoritative 1094-C". Leave Box 19 unchecked on the second 1094-C and skip Parts II, III, and IV.

Q: **What number do I enter on line 20?**
A: Normally, if you only submit one 1094-C for your ALE or ALE member, line 18 and line 20 should be the same number.

Q: **My company isn't part of a larger ALE – do I still need to fill out anything in Section (d) of Part III or Part IV?**
A: No, you can skip those sections.

Q: **My company is part of a controlled group or "Aggregated ALE Group" so I need to check "Yes" on line 21 – but what "Aggregated Group Indicator" do I use in Part III, column (d)?**
A: If you were a member of an aggregated group for the entire calendar year enter "X" in the "All 12 Months" box. If you were a member of an aggregated group for fewer than all 12 months, enter "X" in each month that you were a member of the aggregated group. In either case you also need to complete Part IV, listing the name and EIN of the other aggregated group members (up to a maximum of 30 members).

Q: **What is the purpose of line 22?**
A: Line 22 gives employers the chance to certify that they are eligible for up to four different kinds of relief from ACA regulations. The four types of relief have different requirements and different benefits. A given employer may be eligible for one or more forms of relief so you need to look carefully at each option.

Q: **What do certifications 22A and 22B deal with?**
A: 22A and 22B allow the employer to use simplified methods of reporting. Instead of filling out a Form 1095-C for each employee by January 31, the employer can give (at least certain) employees a generic statement. Note: self-insured employers can't use either of these certifications; also, even if an employer can use a generic statement to give to employees, 1095-C forms still have to be submitted to the IRS.

Q: **What's the advantage of using the relief offered in 22A and 22B?**
A: You gain another two months before you have to send actual 1094-C and 1095-C forms to the IRS, and that extra time could be valuable.

Q: **What about 22C?**
A: 22C provides transition relief for ALEs with less than 99 full-time employees (or their equivalent) or for employers with 100 or more full-time employees (or their equivalent). Employers with 100 or more full-time employees can get an 80-employee discount instead of a 30-employee discount (for 2015) if the IRS assesses a penalty for failing to offer any medical coverage to full-time employees. Employers with 50 to 99 full-time employees can escape any penalties for 2015 if they qualify for this form of transitional relief.

Q: **I have 115 full-time employees in my company and my company is an ALEM – part of an aggregated group. Under 22C does each member of the group get the 80-employee discount?**

A: No, the 80 employee discount has to be shared proportionately between the members of the group.

Q: **I have less than 100 full-time employees and equivalents – how do I qualify for 22C relief?**
A: In order to qualify for 22C relief you have to certify that you meet the following conditions:

- You employed fewer than 100 full-time employees (including full-time equivalents) on business days in 2014.
- During the period from February 9, 2014 through December 31, 2014 you did not reduce the size of your workforce or the overall hours of service of your employees in order to qualify for this transition relief. However, if you reduced the size of your workforce or overall hours of service for bona fide business reasons you are still eligible for 22C relief.
- During the period from February 9, 2014 through December 31, 2015 (or for employers with a non-calendar-year plan, ending on the last day of the 2015 plan year) you don't eliminate or materially reduce the health coverage (if any) that you offered as of February 9, 2014.

Q: **What relief is offered under 22D?**
A: Certification 22D (98% Offer Method) requires the employer to have offered affordable health care coverage providing minimum value to at least 98% of the employees receiving 1095-C forms and minimum essential coverage to their dependents (taking into account all months during which the individuals were employees of the employer and not in a Non-Assessment Period). Employers who meet this requirement don't have to complete the "Full-Time Employee Count" in Part III, column (b) of the authoritative 1094-C form.

Q: **What do I enter in Part III?**
A: If you offered minimum essential coverage to at least 95% of your full-time employees and their dependents in 2016, enter "X" in the "Yes" checkbox on line 23 for the months that you offered that coverage – or enter an "X" in the "Yes" checkbox for "All 12 Months" if you offered that coverage for each month in 2016. For any months that you did not offer minimum essential coverage to at least 95% of your full-time employees and their dependents, mark an "X" in the "No" checkbox (or in the "No" checkbox for "All 12 Months" if you failed to offer that coverage in any month of 2016).

Q: **What do I need to fill out on Part IV?**

A: If you are part of an "Aggregated ALE Group" (companies under a common ownership), you need to enter the name and EIN of the other companies in the aggregated group (up to a maximum of 30 companies).

Affordable Care Act - Form 1095-C

Q: **If an employer is an Applicable Large Employer (ALE) and offers health insurance through an insurance company, what parts of Form 1095-C does that employer have to complete?**
A: An ALE who provides insurance through an insurance company must complete a 1095-C form, Parts I and II, for each full-time employee.

Q: **I had some summer workers who weren't offered health insurance – do I need to send them 1095-C forms?**
A: You need to send a 1095-C to any employee who is considered full-time, regardless of whether or not that person was offered health care coverage.

Q: **If an employer is an ALE and is self-insured, what parts of Form 1095-C does that employer complete?**
A: Self-insured ALEs must complete a 1095-C form (Parts I, II, and III) for each full-time employee and a 1095-C form (Part I, Line 14 of Part II, and Part III) for each non-full-time employee.

Q: **In Part I, it asks for the name and address of my company. My company is part of a controlled group – do I put the name and address of my company or the name and address of our parent company?**
A: Put the legal name and the address of your company, not the parent company's name and address.

Q: **I don't offer health insurance – what do I put in the box "Plan Start Month"?**
A: You can leave that box blank.

Q: **I'm confused – what codes do I use for line 14?**
A: Line 14 is asking what kind, if any, of medical benefits did you offer the particular employee listed on this 1095-C. Here's a list of the codes for line 14 and when to use them:
  - 1A (often used) – Minimum essential coverage providing minimum value offered to a full-time employee (with the employee monthly contribution for the lowest cost self-only coverage equal to or less than 9.5% of the 2014 mainland federal poverty level for a single individual divided by 12) and at least minimum essential coverage offered to the spouse and

dependent(s). Note: the 2014 federal poverty level for a single individual was $11,670.

- 1B (seldom used) - Minimum essential coverage providing minimum value offered to employee only.
- 1C (sometimes used) - Minimum essential coverage providing minimum value offered to employee and at least minimum essential coverage offered to dependent(s) (not spouse).
- 1D (seldom used) - Minimum essential coverage providing minimum value offered to employee and at least minimum essential coverage offered to spouse (not dependent(s)). [Note: 1D is rarely used – if coverage is offered to the employee and spouse, coverage is also normally offered to dependents].
- 1E (often used) - Minimum essential coverage providing minimum value offered to employee and at least minimum essential coverage offered to dependent(s) and spouse (use instead of code 1A if coverage doesn't meet the affordability standard).
- 1F (sometimes used) - Minimum essential coverage NOT providing minimum value offered to employee; employee and spouse or dependent(s); or employee, spouse and dependents.
- 1G (seldom used) - Offer of coverage to employee who was not a full-time employee for any month of the calendar year (which may include one or more months in which the individual was not an employee) and who enrolled in self-insured coverage for one or more months of the calendar year.
- 1H (often used) - No offer of coverage (employee not offered any health coverage or employee offered coverage that is not minimum essential coverage, which may include one or more months in which the individual was not an employee).
- 1I (sometimes used) - Qualifying Offer Transition Relief 2015: Employee (and spouse or dependents) received no offer of coverage; received an offer that is not a qualifying offer; or received a qualifying offer for less than 12 months.

Note: If one of the above codes applies to a particular employee for all 12 months of the year just enter the code once, in the "All 12 months" column.

Q: **I didn't offer one of my employees coverage in January or February because she didn't work for me until March – so what code do I use on line 14?**
A: You use code 1H. Regardless of the reason, you enter 1H for any month that you didn't offer medical benefits to someone you employed during the year.

Q: **What code do I use for months where the employee was in a lawful waiting period?**
A: Again, use code 1H. The reason why you didn't offer medical coverage doesn't matter. However, you can enter 2D on line 16 to indicate that the employee was in a limited non-assessment period and no penalty should be applied. Use the same codes (1H on line 14 and 2D on line 16) if an employee finishes the waiting period and enrolls in coverage in the middle of a month.

Q: **When do I use code 1A versus code 1E?**
A: If you offer a plan to full-time employees and their spouse and dependents that provides minimum value, then you meet the requirements for using code 1E. If, in addition, the employee's monthly contribution is $93.18 or less then you also meet the federal poverty level safe harbor and can use code 1A instead.

Q: **If I offer minimum value coverage to my full-time employees and their dependents and the employee's monthly contribution is $90, do I use code 1A on line 14?**
A: No, code 1A requires that you offer the coverage to the employee and his or her spouse, as well as dependents. In this case since coverage isn't being offered to the spouse, you would use code 1C.

Q: **Do employees in a waiting period (an initial measurement period or a limited non-assessment period) have to be counted in determining whether you offered coverage to 70% of your full-time employees during a given month?**
A: No, employees in a waiting period aren't counted in determining whether an employer offered coverage to at least 70% of full-time employees I

Q: **Do I have to enter the employee share of the lowest cost monthly premium for self-only coverage in every box on line 15?**
A: You only have to enter the employee cost in one of the boxes on line 15 if the line 14 code for that month is 1B, 1C, 1D, or 1E. In fact, if you enter code 1A or code 1I on line 14 be sure not to enter anything on line 15.

Q: **Do I have to fill out the individual boxes on lines 14 and 15 if the medical coverage code and the employee's share of the lowest cost monthly premium amount were the same for all 12 months?**

A: No. Just enter the appropriate code in the "All 12 Months" box on line 14 and the employee's monthly cost in the "All 12 Months" box on line 15.

Q: **We had to lay off an employee at the end of July and she opted for COBRA coverage beginning August 1st. What codes do we use on lines 14, 15 and 16?**
A: Use code 1H on line 14 for August through December (whether or not the terminated employee elects COBRA coverage), leave line 15 blank and enter 2A (not employed) on line 16.

Q: **We didn't offer health insurance to our employees during 2015, but we're claiming Section 4980H(a) transitional relief for employers with 50 to 99 full-time employees in 2015. What codes do we use on lines 14 and 16 on the 1095-C forms?**
A: Use 1H in the "All 12 months" box on line 14. Leave lines 15 and 16 blank.

Q: **Since it's not necessary to provide a 1095-C form to part-time employees, when would you use code 1G?**
A: It's not necessary to report an offer of coverage to a part-time employee if coverage was declined. However, it is necessary to provide a 1095-C for part-time employees actually covered under a self-funded plan. If coverage was offered and accepted than you would use code 1G on line 14 of Part II (leaving lines 15 and 16 blank) and you would complete Part III to indicate which months the individual was actually covered under the self-funded plan.

Q: **Exactly what am I supposed to enter on line 16?**
A: You aren't required to make any entry on line 16 – but you can use line 16 to explain why you didn't offer coverage to an eligible employee or what the employee did after you offered coverage (accepted it, rejected it, etc.).

Q: **What are the codes for line 16?**
A: Here are the codes and when to use them:
- 2A – The employee was not employed during any day of the month.
- 2B – This code is used for several cases:
  - The employee was not a full-time employee for the month and did not enroll in minimum essential coverage (if offered).
  - The employee was a full-time employee during the month but his or her coverage (or offer of coverage) ended before the last day of the month solely because the employee

terminated employment during the month (in other words, the coverage or offer of coverage would have continued if the employee hadn't left).

- Use this code for January 2015 if the employee was offered coverage no later than the first day of the first payroll period in January and the coverage was "affordable" under the ACA rules.
- 2C – Use code 2C for any month in which the employee was enrolled in the coverage offered for each day of the month, regardless of what other codes might apply.
- 2D – Use 2D for any month in which the employee was in a Limited Non-Assessment Period.
- 2E – Use code 2E for any month in which the employer offered health coverage to the employee and was required by a collective bargaining agreement to make contributions for that employee to a multi-employer plan offering affordable, minimum value self-only coverage as well as coverage for the employee's dependents.
- 2F – Use 2F on line 16 for each month if you used the Form W-2 safe harbor to determine affordability for this employee for any month(s).
- 2G – Use 2G on line 16 if you used the federal poverty line safe harbor to determine affordability for this employee for any month(s).
- 2H – Use 2H on line 16 if you used the rate of pay safe harbor to determine affordability for this employee for any month(s).
- 2I – Enter code 2I if non-calendar year transition relief applies to this employee for a given month.

Note: Employers eligible for relief provided in the multi-employer interim guidance for a given month for an employee should use code 2E rather than 2F, 2G or 2H.

Q: **I'm not sure which code to enter on line 16 – what should I do?**
A: If you can't determine which code to use, leave line 16 blank rather than risk using the wrong code.

Q: **What code do I use for an employee who was hired March 15th with coverage offered June 1st after a waiting period of 60 days (with coverage to be offered on the 1st of the month following the 60 days), and the employee waived coverage? (Note: self-only minimum value coverage cost was less than 9.5% of the federal poverty level)**

A: On line 14 use code 1H (no offer of coverage) for January through May and code 1A (offer of coverage at less than 9.5% of FPL) for June through December. No entry is needed on line 15 since the offer is less than 9.5% of the FPL. On line 16, use code 2A for January and February (since the person wasn't employed then), code 2D (employee in waiting period) for March through May, and leave line 16 blank for June through December since the employee declined coverage (if he or she had accepted coverage you would have used code 2C for June through December).

Q: **Our plan year begins on March 1st and we're taking advantage of the non-calendar year plan transition relief by not offering coverage to full-time employees until March 1st. Our lowest-cost self-only coverage plan costs $118 a month. What codes do we use on lines 14, 15 and 16 for an employee who enrolls in coverage on March 1st?**
A: On line 14 use code 1H (no offer of coverage) for January and February, leave line 15 blank for January and February, and use code 2I on line 16 for January and February. Use code 1E (coverage offered) on line 14 for March through December, enter $118 on line 15 for March through December and enter code 2C (employee enrolled in coverage) on line 16 for March through December.

Q: **What codes do I use on lines 14 and 16 for each month for a full-time employee who was enrolled in minimum essential coverage (employee only), left on April 13th, was re-hired on September 2nd and coverage was resumed on October 1st?**
A: Use 1B on line 14 and 2C on line 16 for January, February, and March, code 1H on line 14 and 2B on line 16 for April and code 1H on line 14 and 2A on line 16 for May, June, July, and August. Then use 1B on line 14 and 2C on line 16 for October, November and December.

Q: **If a full-time employee leaves and is re-hired within 13 weeks can I wait 90 days to offer health care coverage?**
A: Under ACA rules, rehires who have been gone less than 13 weeks have to be offered coverage no later than the first of the month following their rehire date. (Note: Your insurance provider may specify that the employee has to go through an entire waiting period again).

Q: **I've finished with line 16 – now what?**
A: If you buy insurance coverage from an insurance company you're done. However, if you're self-insured you need to go ahead and fill out Part III which asks for information on covered employees (name, Social Security number, date of birth, and months of coverage).

Reporting Health Care Costs on the W-2

If you have 250 or more employees you are required to report the total value of certain employer-sponsored health benefits on your employees' W-2 forms (you may also choose to report that amount even if you have less than 250 employees). There are three main methods that can be used to calculate the value of health care benefits:

1) Premium charged method: The amount that goes on the W-2 is simply the premium the insurer charges for the employee's health care coverage for the year (this method can only be used for an employee covered by the employer's group health plan).
2) COBRA premium method: This method must be used for self-insured health care plans. The employer calculates the applicable COBRA premiums, excluding the 2 percent COBRA administrative fee and uses the amount on the employee's W-2.
3) Modified COBRA premium method: Employers can use this method if they subsidize the cost of COBRA coverage. The amount used on the W-2 is calculated based on a reasonable estimate of the COBRA premium if the estimate is used to establish the subsidized COBRA premium.

Note: Employers are not required to include standalone dental and vision plans when calculating the the reportable health care costs.

Outsourcing

Q: We're spending too much time on payroll -- what can we do about it?
A: Payroll and Human Resource functions can eat up a good deal of time -- time that you, as an employer, would much rather spend doing whatever it is you're in business to do. Not only that, IRS has reported that 40% of small businesses that handle their own payrolls are fined for inaccurate returns. If you can cost justify it, outsourcing your payroll can be a real time saver as well as reducing the number of things you have to worry about. Professional payroll processing companies have a variety of services available for employers. You can let them handle everything from payroll input to tax deposits to filing of forms or you can do the input, employee updates, tax deposits and quarterly/annual reports in-house if you want greater control over the payroll process. In either case, look for a company that does payroll as it's main function, find out if they have clients with businesses similar to yours, be sure to check out the references they give you, and make certain you have a firm quote as to what you're going to be charged.

Q: What about using payroll software?
A: Almost all payroll services provide software packages that you can install and run on your own PC as a front-end to their system. Some payroll processors also offer an online option that allows you to do almost everything on the internet, using just your browser. What if you just want to do your payroll in-house, without using a payroll company? Well, there are many different software packages on the market that you can choose from, including Intuit's QuickBooks payroll, Sage Systems Abra payroll, Cougar Mountain payroll, Pensoft Payroll Plus, CheckMark Software's Payroll for Windows, Red Wing payroll, and many others. You can find descriptions and ratings for these packages at various sites on the internet (www.cpatechnologyadvisor.com for example).

Getting Help

Q: **Where can I find help from IRS with payroll questions?**
A: Here are a few of the publications that IRS provides containing information on payroll taxes and reports:

- IRS Publication 15 (Circular E) – Employers Tax Guide (www.irs.gov/pub/irs-pdf/p15.pdf)
- IRS Publication 15a – Employers Supplemental Tax Guide (www.irs.gov/pub/irs-pdf/p15a.pdf)
- IRS Publication 15b – Employers Guide to Fringe Benefits (www.irs.gov/pub/irs-pdf/p15b.pdf)

Q: **What about information from the Social Security Administration?**
A: www.ssa.gov/employer/ provides information on W-2 filing and Social Security number verification.

Q: **Where can I get advice about federal employment laws?**
A: The Department of Labor has created a group of online "advisors" (or "elaws") to help employers understand their rights and responsibilities under federal employment laws. The "elaws" cover a number of subjects including pay and overtime, employee benefits, and safety and health issues. The elaws are interactive tools designed to provide the same sort of advice you would get from an employment law expert. You can access the elaws at http://www.dol.gov/elaws.

Q: **What about payroll guides?**
A: Aspen Publishers (www.aspenpublishers.com) offers a number of publications by Wolters & Kluwer dealing with payroll and human resources. Their products include:

- *American Payroll Association (APA) Basic Guide to Payroll, 2017 Edition*
- *Multistate Payroll Guide, 2017 Edition*
- *U.S. Master Payroll Guide*
- *Wage and Hour Answer Book, 2017 Edition*
- *Wage-Hour Compliance Handbook, 2017 Edition*
- *Payroll Manager's Newsletter*
- *Complete Guide to Federal & State Garnishment, 2017 Edition*
- *Payroll Answer Book*
- *Quick Reference to Payroll Compliance*

Q: **What about payroll forums?**
A: Payroll forums and discussion groups include:

- www.payrolltalk.com – Discussions on payroll and human resources topics.
- www.payroll-taxes.com – Help with federal and state tax questions.
- www.taxforums.us/f-payroll-tax-forum-23.html – Discussions about payroll taxes and tax forms.

Q: **What about payroll blogs?**
A: There are some helpful blogs although most of them are connected to a specific payroll or payroll provider:
- www.hrpayrollsystems.net/hrblog/ - Human resources information.
- Www.apspayroll.com/aps-blog/ - General payroll information.
- www.gtm.com/home/blog/ - General payroll information.
- www.blog.adp.com/category/payroll/ - General payroll information.
- Https://cs.thomsonreuters.com/blogs?tag=the%20payroll%20report – General payroll & accounting information.

Security

Q: What should I do about keeping our payroll information secure?
A: There are some general guidelines of course: limit access to payroll data, keep payroll records under lock and key, possibly even move archived payroll information to an outside storage location. If you're using pre-printed checks be sure to audit your checks periodically to make sure that all the unused checks are accounted for and in sequence. Using computerized time clocks and direct deposit can also help keep your payroll information free from tampering. And outsourcing your payroll also offers some advantages in that your payroll provider normally has your payroll information backed up on their system, in case of fire, flood, or some other disaster that could destroy your in-house data.

Q: What about protecting computerized payroll records?
A: Securing payroll data kept on computers is becoming more complicated all the time, especially if the data is on computers that are connected to the internet. Any computer with internet access needs to have a firewall up and running as well as real-time virus and malware scanning software. If you are transmitting payroll data over the web, encrypt that information if at all possible. Also, if you send ACH (Automated Clearing House) files such as direct deposit files via the internet, be sure to set up a verification process with the financial institution receiving the files to make sure that when they receive a file it's actually one that you sent.

Closing Your Business

Q: What do I need to do if I'm closing my business?
A: There are a number of steps you need to take to close down your business properly:

- Collect any outstanding accounts receivable
- Notify your creditors
- Notify your customers/clients and fulfill any remaining contractual obligations
- Notify your employees and make plans to pay your employees on the last day of business (including accrued vacation time)
- Sell off inventory
- Terminate your lease(s)
- Liquidate your business assets
- Settle your debts (at least as much as possible)
- Cancel business credit cards
- Close your business bank account(s)
- Cancel state or county licenses and permits
- Run your final payroll, distribute employee copies of W-2s and make your final federal and state payroll tax deposits
- Distribute 1099-MISC forms to vendors/sub-contractors
- File your final quarterly and annual employment tax forms (940, 941, 943. 943-A, W-2s and 1099s, Form 8027 (Annual Return of Tip Income and Allocated Tips), and state and local reporting forms.
- Report capital gains and losses:
  - Form 1040 – Individual tax return
  - Form 1065 – U.S. Partnership Return of Income
  - Form 1120 Schedule D – Capital gains and losses.
- Report partner's/shareholder's shares:
  - Form 1065 (Schedule K-1)
  - Form 1120 (Schedule K-1)
- File final employee pension/benefit plan (Form 5500)
- Distribute any remaining assets to yourself and any other owners
- Formally dissolve your partnership, corporation or LLC, filing the required forms (Fomr 966 – Corporate Dissolution or Liquidation)
- Consider allowing S corporation election to terminate (Form 1120S instructions)
- Report business asset sales (Form 8594 – Asset Acquisition Statement

- Report the sale or exchange of property used in your trade or business (Form 4797 – Sales of Business Property)

Miscellaneous

Q: **What do I need to know about workers' comp insurance?**
A: Workers Compensation Insurance is a system to provide medical care and compensation to workers who become ill from work-related causes or are injured on the job. The system usually operates by means of mandatory insurance coverage imposed on employers. Policies include two separate coverages: workers' compensation and employers liability. The insurer (state agency or private company) will pay benefits to employees for sickness or injury incurred on the job and the liability portion of the coverage protects the employer for employee work-related bodily injury that doesn't fall under workers' compensation coverage. Before you go looking for workers' comp coverage (assuming you're in a state that allows employers to deal with private insurance companies) you need to know your estimated payroll for the coming year so the insurance agent can determine the amount of coverage your company needs. You will also need job descriptions for all your employees for classification purposes -- you'll pay a higher premium for a construction worker than you would for a secretary.

Q: **How are a company's workers' compensation insurance premiums calculated?**
A: Premiums are calculated according to the job classifications of the company's employees, the size of the organization's payroll and the company's experience modification factor or "MOD" (which is based on the organization's record of job-related accidents and illnesses). Different job classifications are assigned a dollar rate based on the risk factor involved in that job and the rates vary by state. In a typical state for example, the dollar rate for a clerical worker may be 20 cents per $100 of payroll, while the rate for a carpenter working in residential construction might be $8.21 per $100 of payroll. The amount of a company's insurance premium is equal to the total over all the company's job classifications of the wages paid to workers in each classification (divided by $100) times the rate for that classification times the company's experience modification factor.

Q: **What is the employer's responsibility for providing medical treatment for an employee's job-related injury?**
A: Employers are responsible for arranging immediate medical treatment as soon as the employee notifies them of the injury (Note: in most states the employee has to inform the employer of the illness or injury within a certain period of time – usually from 7 to 30 days). Once informed of the

injury or illness the employer is also required to provide the employee with a claim form to fill out so the claim can be submitted to the workers' compensation insurance provider. Depending on the state, the injured employee may have to select from a network of physicians provided by the insurance company or, If the employee selected a personal physician in a written notice to the employer prior to any injury or illness, he or she may be able to go to that physician for treatment immediately after an injury.

Q: If an employee leaves do I have to pay him severance pay?
A: The Fair Labor Standards Act (FLSA) requires an employer to pay an employee who has been terminated his or her regular wages through the employee's termination date and for any time the person has accrued (accrued time usually includes vacation or personal days but not sick days). Severance pay however, unless specifically provided for in the employment contract, is up to the good will of the employer. If you do offer severance pay it may be a good idea to ask the employee to sign a release from any future claims in return for accepting the severance pay (Note: If the employee is 40 or older the "Older Workers' Benefits Protection Act" dictates what must be included in the release).

Q: What is "Escheatment"?
A: Escheatment has to do with unclaimed payroll checks. An employee never gives up his or her right to a wage payment, no matter how long that payment goes unclaimed. After a certain length of time -- in most states, one year -- uncollected wages are considered to be abandoned and the employer is obligated to turn them over to the state, which holds the money in custody for the payee (the actual transfer of funds to the state is the escheatment process). The state keeps these funds on behalf of the owner but can use the money however it wants to until the owner actually comes to collect it -- which means that state governments are often actively checking on employers to make sure that they are turning over all unclaimed funds in a timely manner.

Q: What do I do about an unclaimed employee paycheck?
A: See "escheatment" above.

Q: What is "COBRA"?
A: The Consolidated Omnibus Budget Reconciliation Act of 1985 requires employers who sponsor employee health plans to provide workers and their dependents and beneficiaries with the opportunity to keep continued group health coverage for a given period of time if their coverage is lost due to certain "qualifying events". The continuation coverage must be the same as that provided to workers still on the

payroll. Qualifying events include the death of an employee, termination of the employee or reduction of the employee's hours (other than for gross misconduct), divorces involving a covered dependent, and several other situations. The continuation period is usually either 18 or 36 months and the employer must provide the recipient an option to switch to individual coverage before the continuation period runs out.

Q: **Are all employers with group health care plans subject to COBRA?**
A: Only employers with 20 or more employees on more than 50 percent of its typical business days in the previous calendar year are subject to COBRA. Note: Part-time employees count as a fraction of an employee with the fraction equal to the the number of hours the part-time employee worked divided by the number of hours a full-time employee would have worked.

Q: **What is "COBRA Premium Assistance"?**
Note: COBRA Premium Assistance expired as of February 2012.
A: The American Recovery and Reinvestment Act (ARRA) of 2009 provides for premium reductions for COBRA health benefits. Eligible individuals pay only 35% of their COBRA premiums and their insurance provider (you, the employer in this case) pays the other 65% which is reimbursed to you as a tax credit on the Form 941 (Employer's Quarterly Federal Tax Return) or Form 944 (Employer's Annual Federal Tax Return). The premium reduction applies to periods of health coverage that began after February 17, 2009 and lasts for 15 months. To qualify, individuals must have experienced one of the qualifying events listed above (under "What is COBRA") and the event must have taken place from September 1, 2008 through May 31, 2010.

Q: **What does "Gross Up" mean?**
A: If an employer wants to pay an employee's taxes for him (on a Christmas bonus check for example), then the net pay has to be "grossed up" to include the tax amounts the employer paid. For example, you would take the percentage of wages that goes for Social Security (.062) plus the percentage for Medicare (.0145) plus some reasonable percentage for federal income tax (.2500) plus a percentage for state income tax (.0800) and add those percentages together (.4065); then divide that percentage into 1.0000 and multiply the net pay by the result to get the correct gross pay. If the employer is taking FICA taxes only, you can divide the net pay by .9235 to get the "bumped up" gross pay.

Q: **What is the normal length of a "pay period"?**

A: Pay periods are usually weekly, bi-weekly (every two weeks), semi-monthly (twice a month), or monthly. In any case a pay period cannot be longer than 31 consecutive days.

Payroll Quiz

1) What is the current federal minimum wage?
   A) $5.15 per hour
   B) $5.75 per hour
   C) $8.50 per hour
   D) $7.25 per hour
2) The tax paid by the employer that amounts to 0.6% of each employee's first $7,000 of annual wages is called _____ tax.
3) An employee is paid $12.50 per hour (time and a half for overtime) and during the past week the employee worked 52 hours. What are the employee's gross wages for the week?
4) Cafeteria plan contributions are federal income taxable (True/False)
5) According to IRS statutes, to qualify as part-time an employee should work no more than __ hours per week.
   A) 20
   B) 29
   C) 30
   D) 32
6) The combination of Social Security tax and Medicare tax is referred to as _____ tax
7) For 2017 the Social Security tax rate for employees is _____
8) The 2017 wage limit for Social Security withholding is:
   A) $118,500
   B) $118,700
   C) $106,800
   D) $117,000
   E) $127,200
9) What is the total amount of employer and employee FICA tax liability in 2017 for an employee with gross FICA taxable wages of $205,000?
10) ABC Company has a employee named Adam who makes $820 a week. For last week ABC made the following payroll calculations for Adam: $825 gross pay, $63.11 for FICA withholding, $76.00 for Federal Income Tax withholding, $37.00 for state income tax withholding, and $40 due for federal and state unemployment taxes
   .A) If Adam has no other deductions what is his net pay for the week?
   B) What is ABC's total expense for Adam for the week?
11) 401(k) contributions are:
   A) FICA taxable but not federal or state taxable

B) FICA, federal and state taxable
C) Exempt from FICA, federal and state withholding
D) FICA and federal taxable, but not state taxable

12) The 940 Federal Unemployment Tax Return is submitted:
A) Quarterly
B) Yearly
C) Monthly

13) What determines whether a person is an independent contractor or an employee?

14) ABC Company is using a person from a temporary help agency to fill in for an employee on maternity leave – does that person become an employee of ABC Company?

15) If ABC Company has an employee who works in one state and lives in another does ABC have to take out withholding tax for the employee's state of residence?

16) ABC Company wants to give each employee a $500 bonus – what amount should each person be paid so that the net after deducting FICA tax equals $500?

17) ABC's most recent payroll had a check date of Friday, February 18 – Monday the 21st is a federal holiday – ABC (a semi-weekly depositor) should make the federal tax deposit by what date?

18) How can ABC Company get reimbursed for COBRA premium assistance payments?

19) In March ABC Company transferred Mary Sanders from state X to state Y. At the end of the year she had been paid $4,600 in state X and $31,200 in state Y. ABC has an SUI rate in state Y of 3.5% and state Y has an SUI wage limit of $7000, while state X has an SUI wage limit of $9500. How much does ABC Company owe in SUTA tax to state Y for Mary Sanders?

20) What is the maximum amount Ron Norvil (age 49) can contribute to ABC Company's 401(k) plan in 2017?

21) What form is used to apply to IRS for an employer identification number?

22) Use the following information for questions 22 -24: An employee worked the entire year in 2016 and earned two weeks of vacation as specified in the company's policies manual. The policy manual also states that amount paid will be 80 hours times the employee's rate of pay as of December 31, 2016. At that time the employee's pay rate was $15 per hour. Which financial statements are affected in 2016? (Balance Sheet only, Income Statement only, Balance Sheet and Income Statement, Neither the Balance Sheet or Income Statement)?

23) The amount that will be reported on the 2017 income statement as Vacation Expense for the vacation earned in 2016 is _____?

24) When the employer pays the employee for the vacation earned in 2016, what account will be debited (Cash, Vacation Expense, or Vacation Payable)?

25) In January an employer remits the state unemployment tax that pertains to its employees' wages for the final quarter of 2016. On which income statement will the state unemployment tax appear under accrual accounting?

26) If an employee who is paid weekly makes $14 an hour and is also being paid $500 a month for housing, how much should he be paid for working 45 hours last week?

27) ABC Company wants to pay each shop employee a bonus of $500 - each person will have FICA taxes taken out but no federal, state, or local withholding tax. What should the gross amount of each bonus be if the employees are to get exactly $500?

28) Do W-4 forms have to be submitted to the IRS?

29) Do you need to file a form 940 quarterly?

30) Can IRS penalize an employer for failing to obtain an employee's Social Security number?

31) If an employee is paid weekly and has disposable earnings (earnings after taxes) of $285 per week, what portion of the disposable earnings can be garnished?

32) If an employee regularly takes 30 minute coffee breaks do I have to count that half hour as hours worked?

33) Do I have to pay extra to employees who are working a night shift?

34) You have a non-exempt employee (i.e., an employee subject to overtime rules) who is being paid a salary of $550 per week. If that person worked 48 hours last week how much should he be paid?

35) A restaurant includes a charge on the tip line of its bills equal to 10% of the total charges for food and beverages. Does the server need to include that charge in his or her record of tips received?

36) Janice Doe's taxable earnings for the current payroll amounts to $3,500 which will increase her year-to-date FICA taxable earnings to $201,500 - how much will her Social Security and Medicare taxes be for this payroll? How much will her employer have to pay in matching FICA tax for Janice?

37) Mindy made $18 in tips this month – are those tips taxable and does she need to report them to her employer?

38) What does the Fair Labor Standards Act say about an employee's paid time off?

39) If IRS advises you that an employee's W-4 if invalid you should:

A) Take no action.
B) Have the employee fill out a new W-4 and send it to the IRS.
C) Withhold taxes for the employee based on the information provided by the IRS.

40) Karen is paid $12 per hour. During the past week she worked 24 hours on day shift and 24 hours on night shift (which pays an additional $1.00 per hour). How much should Karen's gross pay be for the week?

41) How long should an employer keep records about an employee who took leave based on the Family and Medical Leave Act?

42) True or False – An employee who is paid a salary is automatically exempt from minimum wage and overtime rules.

43) Jonathan is a nonexempt employee and is paid $525 per week for a 35 hour workweek. If he works 50 hours during a given week, what should his gross pay be for the week?

44) You want to pay Marion a net bonus of $2000 (YTD gross earnings are $22,000). Using the current flat rate of 25% for supplemental wages and assuming that the only other taxes are for Social Security and Medicare, what should be the gross amount of Marion's bonus check?

45) Are workers compensation payments taxable?

46) Tim works for two employers and, as a result of taxes being taken out by each employer, has overpaid on social security tax. Can he ask for a refund from either or both employers?

47) Janice's gross pay for the (semi-monthly) pay period is $1,835 and she has a cafeteria plan deduction of $60 and a 401(k) deduction of $40. Assuming there is no state tax, that Janice claims married and zero deductions on her W-4, and that her YTD gross is $25,750, what should her net pay be for the pay period?

48) If you provide severance pay as a separate check for a terminated employee how should you calculate the amount of federal income tax to be withheld?

49) How much will Tom's employer have *remitted* in FICA taxes for Tom if Tom ends up with $50,000 in FICA taxable earnings for 2014? What if Tom's FICA taxable earnings for the year is $205,000?

50) If a new employee is in the United States on an H1-B visa, what taxes need to be taken out of his or her pay?

51) What is the total cost of my payroll?

52) An employee only needs to change his or her W-4 if there's a change in filing status or exemptions – True or False?

53) What form is used to apply for a Social Security number?

54) To qualify as an "exempt" employee for overtime purposes a workers must be paid on a salary basis at not less than _____ per week.
55) If the IRS determines that an employee doesn't have enough federal income tax withheld what will it ask an employee to do?
56) Can a temporary employee hired through a "temp" agency participate in the company's pension plan?
57) Do "temp" workers count as "employees" of the business they're working for under the Affordable Care Act?
58) Which federal taxes are an employee's final wages subject to after his or her death?
59) A salaried-exempt employee is unable to work for two days during the work week because the office is closed due to a water leak. The employee's weekly guaranteed salary is $800. Under FLSA rules what amount must the employee be paid for the work week?
   A) $600
   B) $750
   C) $800
   D) $400
60) Which of the following individuals would most likely be classified as an independent contractor: a salesman working from home, a repairman called in on a regular schedule to service the company's PCs, or a person who normally works in the shipping department but comes in after hours to clean the offices.
61) Can a Cafeteria (Section 125) plan offer a deferred pay benefit?
62) Which of the following has to be determined before overtime calculations can be done for an employee:
      a) the employee's marital status
      b) the company's workweek
      c) the employee's pay frequency
63) What is "imputed income" and is it taxable?
64) Can an employee select both a pre-tax and a post-tax item from the company's list of Section 125 cafeteria plan options?
65) Which worker would be considered a statutory employee: a) real estate agent, b) full-time life insurance salesperson, c) accountant

Payroll Quiz Answers

1) D - $7.25 per hour
2) Federal Unemployment Tax
3) $725 (40 hours at $12.50/hour + 12 hours of overtime at time and a half or $18.75/hour)
4) False (in general) – Cafeteria plan insurance is exempt from both FICA and federal income tax (and in most cases, state income tax) unless the employee chooses to have the deduction treated as post-tax (after taxes have been taken).
5) B – Employees who work 30 or more hours a week are generally considered to be full time.
6) FICA (Federal Insurance Contributions Act) tax
7) 6.2 %
8) E - $127,200
9) $21,762.80 (127,200 x .062 + 200,000 x .0145 + 5,000 x .0235 for the employee + 127,200 x .062 + 205,000 x .0145 for the employer share)
10) A - Adam's net pay = $648.89 ($825.00 – $63.11 – $76.00 – $37.00). FUI and SUI taxes are paid entirely by the employer (except in Alaska, New Jersey or Pennsylvania which assess unemployment taxes on employees).
B) $928.11 ($825 gross pay + $825 x .0765 for the employer's FICA match + $40 for unemployment taxes paid by the employer)
11) A – FICA taxable but not federal or state taxable
12) B – the 940 form is submitted annually (and is due by the end of January of the next year).
13) If the employer has the right to control not only what work will be done but how and when, then the worker is effectively an employee rather than an independent contractor
14) No, the person is still employed by the temporary help agency
15) ABC Company isn't required to do so, but if the state where the person works and the state where he or she resides have a "reciprocity" agreement, ABC can elect to deduct state tax for the state of residence.
16) Assuming no employee has more than $127,200 in FICA taxable earnings for the year, each person should be paid $541.42 ($500 = Gross – Gross x .0765 or Gross = $500 / .9235)
17) ABC should make the tax deposit by Thursday the 24th (the third working day following the check date)
18) COBRA assistance payments can be entered and applied as a tax credit on the 941 quarterly tax return.

19) $84.00 ($7,000 - $4,600 = $2400; $2400 x .035 = $84.00). Note: Louisiana, Minnesota and Montana don't allow carry-over of SUI wages – if Mary had been transferred to one of those states ABC Company would owe $245 ($7000 x .035).

20) $18,000 unless Ron turns 50 during 2017 – in that case he could contribute up to $24,000.

21) Form SS-4 (Application for Employer Identification Number)

22) Both the Income Statement and the Balance Sheet – an entry will be made to Vacation Expense on the 2016 income statement and an offsetting entry will be made to Vacation Payable on the 2016 balance sheet.

23) Zero – the cost of the vacation pay will be an expense on the 2016 income statement.

24) Vacation Payable will be debited.

25) Under accrual accounting the state unemployment tax expense will appear on the 2016 income statement.

26) The value of the housing allowance has to be added to the employee's wages for the workweek in order to calculate a regular rate of pay. To do that, multiply $500 by 12 and divide by 52 to get the weekly value of the housing - that total is $115.38. Add the weekly value of the housing to the employee's straight time wages of 45 hours x $14 per hour: $115.38 + $630.00 = $745.38. Divide $745.38 by the number of hours worked last week to get an effective rate of pay: $745.38 / 45 = $16.56. Assuming an overtime factor of 1.5, the employee's overtime pay would be 5 hours (the excess over 40 hours) x $16.56 x 1.5 which equals $124.20. Then the employee's total pay would be the effective rate of pay times 40 hours plus the overtime pay or $16.56 x 40 = $662.40 plus $124.20, which equals $786.60.

27) To "gross up" the amount of each pay check to cover FICA taxes you divide the amount of the bonus by 100% minus the FICA percentage. Assuming all the shop employees are under the Social Security wage limit, you would divide $500 by 1.0000 minus .0765 (which equals .9235), giving a gross amount of $541.42.

28) No. W-4 forms should be kept in the employee's file in case there is a question about their withholding tax.

29) No, Form 940 is an annual form, filed by the end of January for the preceding year. However, if your FUTA tax is $500 or more for the year you need to make quarterly FUTA payments.

30) There is no direct penalty, but the employer can be penalized for submitting incorrect or incomplete information returns such as W-2s.

31) $67.50 can be garnished (the amount by which disposable earnings exceeds the federal minimum wage of $7.25 per hour times 30 or $217.50). If the amount of disposable earnings was $290 or more then the garnishment couldn't exceed 25% times the disposable earnings, since that amount would be less than the difference between disposable earnings and $217.50.

32) Under FLSA rules, if the employer has expressly communicated to employees that work breaks may only last for up to 20 minutes, then you only need to count 20 or those 30 minutes as hours worked.

33) No, you don't have to pay extra for working a night shift – that's strictly a matter of agreement between employer and employees.

34) To calculate the employee's overtime pay divide the weekly salary by the number of hours the individual is expected to work in one week. Then multiply the resulting hourly rate by 1.5 and multiply that figure by the number of overtime hours worked: $550 / 40 hours = $13.75 per hour x 1.5 x 8 hours = $165.00 The total gross pay would be $550 + $165 = $715.00.

35) No, since the customer didn't have the right to determine the amount on the "tip line", the 10% charge is considered wages not tips.

36) Janice's Social Security tax will be zero since her FICA taxable wages were already over the $127,200 wage limit for 2017. Since the Medicare tax rate increases from 1.45% to 2.35% when an individual's taxable earnings reach $200,000, Janice's Medicare tax will be $3500 x .0145 + $1500 (the amount of FICA taxable wages over $200,000) x .009 which equals $50.75 + $13.50 or $64.25. Her employer's matching FICA tax for Janice will be $50.75 ($3500 x .0145) – since the additional Medicare tax applies to the employee only.

37) No. You must make at least $20 a month in tips for the tips to be taxable – tips of less than $20 in a month don't need to be reported to the employer.

38) The FLSA (Fair Labor Standards Act) covers overtime pay, minimum wage, and minimum age of workers but it doesn't cover paid time off.

39) C – withhold taxes based on the information provided by the IRS.

40) Karen's gross pay for the week is $650. Her straight time earnings are: 24 hours x $12/hour for the day shifts plus 24 hours x $13/hour for the night shifts or $600. To calculate her overall earnings you have to determine her "regular rate of pay" which equals her straight time earnings divided by the total hours worked or $600 / 48 hours, which equals $12.50 per hour. Then

her total gross pay is 40 hours x $12.50 plus 8 hours x $18.75 ($12.50 at time and a half), or $650.00.

41) Records concerning instances of an employee taking leave time under the Family and Medical Leave Act should be kept for at least 3 years.

42) False. Just because an employee is paid a salary doesn't automatically exempt him or her from minimum wage and overtime rules. The employee also has to meet specific job duty tests (and make at least $23,600 per year) in order to be considered "exempt".

43) Jonathan's gross pay is based on his "regular hourly rate" which is $525 divided by 35 hours or $15.00 per hour. For a 50 hour workweek Jonathan would be paid for 40 hours at $15.00 per hour and for 10 overtime hours at $22.50 (1 ½ times $15.00), or a total gross pay of $825.00.

44) The total tax percentage on Marion's bonus is .25 + 6.2 + 1.45 or .3265 (the supplemental federal withholding percentage plus the social security percentage plus the Medicare percentage). Then Marion's gross pay minus .3265 x her gross pay has to equal $2,000 – so her gross pay amount is $2,000 divided by (1 - .3265) which equals $2,969.56.

45) Except in certain special cases workers compensation payments to an employee are not considered taxable by the IRS.

46) No. Tim can get his overpayment refunded by claiming the overpayment as a credit on his year-end tax return.

47) Janice's net pay for the pay period is $1,429.56. Her Social Security and Medicare tax is $135.79 ($1,835 minus the $60 pre-tax cafeteria deduction times .0765). Her federal withholding tax is $165.69 (calculated from the federal tax tables as semi-monthly withholding for married individuals with zero deductions, based on gross taxable pay of $1,835 minus the pre-tax $60 cafeteria deduction and minus the pre-tax $40 401(k) deduction). Janice's net pay then is equal to $1,835 - $60 - $40 - $135.79 - $165.69 or $1,429.56.

48) The IRS considers severance pay provided in a separate check to be supplemental income and the federal withholding tax for that payment should be calculated as 25% of the gross taxable wages.

49) $7,650. Tom's employer has to remit Tom's Social Security and Medicare tax ($50,000 times .0765 = $3,825) plus the employer's matching share of $3,825. If Tom's FICA taxable earnings total $205,000, his employer has to remit the employer share ($127,200 in Social Security earnings times .062 + $205,000 times .0145 = $10,226.50). Tom however will have to pay

$10,271.50 - $10,226.50 plus $5,000 times .009 for the Additional Medicare Tax on FICA wages over $200,000.

50) H-visa holders are not exempt from FICA or federal withholding taxes so the normal social security, Medicare and federal withholding tax should be taken out of the employee's pay.

51) The total cost of payroll to an employer is the sum of the gross pay (which covers net pay, voluntary deductions, company contributions and employee Social Security, Medicare, federal, state and any local withholding) plus the employer's matching share of Social Security and Medicare withholding plus federal and state unemployment taxes. Note: depending on the state where the employer does business, there may also be additional taxes such as disability or employee state unemployment withholding.

52) False. If an employee claims exemption from federal withholding on the W-4, that exemption expires at the end of January each year. If a new W-4 isn't submitted by the employee by February 15th IRS regulations require the employer to change the person's tax status to "single" and "zero exemptions" until a new form is received.

53) Form SS-1.

54) To be classified as exempt an employee must be paid a salary of not less than $455 per week (Note: the exempt threshold may change to $913 per week if the Department of Labor's new overtime regulation actually goes into effect at some point).

55) The IRS will send a "lock-in" letter to the employer specifying the maximum number of withholding allowances the employee can claim. Within 60 days from receipt of the letter the employer must begin withholding federal income tax for the employee as indicated in the lock-in letter. From that point the employer can't decrease the employee's withholding unless the IRS approves it.

56) Even employees classified as temporary can participate in an employer's pension plan after completing 1,000 hours of service within a 12-month period.

57) Workers hired through a temporary staffing agency for short-term assignments are presumed to be employees of the staffing agency. However, temporary workers who have more than a short-term assignment with an employer are generally considered employees of that business, not the staffing agency, and must be included in the monthly employee counts and offered appropriate healthcare coverage.

58) Social Security, Medicare and FUTA (Federal Unemployment Tax), but not Federal Income Tax.

59) $800. Under FLSA rules an exempt employee must be paid his regular salary for a given work week regardless of how much he worked during the week- unless he misses the entire work week or voluntarily takes one or more days off.
60) The repairman.
61) In general, no. The only exception is a 401(k) plan.
62) The company's workweek. Under FLSA rules, a workweek is defined as seven consecutive 24-hour periods. The only other requirement is that the day of the week that the workweek starts stays the same and that the workweek is a fixed and regularly-occurring period of 168 hours. Once the workweek that applies to overtime calculations is defined, then the hours worked by the employee can be determined.
63) Imputed income is the value of cash or non-cash employee compensation. Examples of imputed income include: dependent care assistance or adoption assistance that exceeds the tax-free amount, group term taxable life insurance coverage over $50,000, personal use of an employer-provided vehicle, and non-deductible moving expense reimbursements. For payroll purposes imputed income is subject to FICA withholding but not federal income tax withholding (although an employee can elect to have federal income tax withheld) and must be reported as income in boxes on the employee's W-2.
64) Yes, an employee can select both pre-tax and [post-tax items from the company's Section 125 cafeteria plan options.
65) A full-time life insurance salesperson.

Appendix A – Useful Links

http://www.irs.gov (the Internal Revenue Service website - you can find forms, publications and additional payroll information here.
http://www.ssa.gov (the Social Security Administration web site)
http://www.payroll-taxes.com (payroll tax information, check calculators, a tax calendar and a discussion board)
http://www.irs.gov/pub/irs-pdf/f941.pdf (fillable Form 941 – Employer's Quarterly Federal Tax Return)
http://www.irs.gov/pub/irs-pdf/f941x.pdf (fillable Form 941-X Adjusted Employer's Quarterly Federal Tax Return or Claim for Refund)
http://www.irs.gov/pub/irs-pdf/f943.pdf (fillable Form 943 - Employer's Annual Federal Tax Return for Agricultural Employees)
http://www.irs.gov/pub/irs-pdf/f944.pdf (fillable Form 944 - Employer's Annual Federal Tax Return)
http://www.irs.gov/pub/irs-pdf/f940.pdf (fillable Form 940 – Employer's Annual Federal Unemployment Tax Return)

Appendix B – Glossary of Terms

125 Plan: Also known as a "Cafeteria Plan" or "Flex Plan" (see "Cafeteria Plan").

401(k) Plan: An employer sponsored retirement plan which allows employees to contribute part of their wages to the plan each pay period. Employee contributions (and employer matching amounts, if any) are not subject to federal income tax (and most state income taxes) until the money is withdrawn by the employee.

403(b) Plan: A tax advantaged savings plan covering self-employed ministers or employees of a public educational institution, a cooperative hospital service organization, or certain non-profit employers (Internal Revenue Code 501(c)(3) organizations). Tax treatment is similar to a 401(k) plan.

457 Plan: A retirement plan in the form of an annuity or mutual fund for employees of state and local governments and for tax exempt organizations.

1099: IRS forms used to report various types of income other than wages, salaries and tips on an annual basis (similar to W-2 forms). 1099 forms are normally used in connection with payroll to record payments made to independent contractors.

ABA number (routing number): A nine-digit number created by the American Bankers Association that identifies a specific bank or other financial institution within the United States. An ABA number is used for wires and electronic automatic clearing house (ACH) transactions such as direct deposit files and tax payments.

Abate: A term that means to decrease or diminish. Normally used in payroll in reply to a notification of penalty from IRS or some other agency, asking for a cancellation or reduction of the penalty.

Accelerated Deposit Rule: Also known as the "one-day" rule, it requires employers who accumulate a tax liability of $100,000 or more during a pay period to deposit the withheld taxes on the next banking day after the pay date.

AccuWage: A software program available from the Social Security Administration that can be used to test your electronic W-2 file for correct formatting before submitting the file to the SSA.

ACH: Automated Clearing House. A Federal Reserve Bank acting on behalf of an association of financial institutions. The Federal Reserve Bank serves as a clearinghouse for direct deposit or other electronic payment transactions, receiving and transmitting entries. Funds moving from Bank A to Bank B muse go through the Automated Clearing House.

Actual Deferred Percentage (ADP): The percentage of wages deferred by employees under a salary deduction plan such as a 401(k) plan. The ADP percentage is reviewed to determine if a plan meets IRS qualification requirements.

Advanced Earned Income Credit (AEIC): Starting January 1, 2011 advance EIC payments will no longer be made to employees through payroll – employees who are eligible for the Earned Income Credit can still claim the credit when they file their year-end income tax return.

After-tax deduction: A deduction from an employee's pay that does not reduce the employee's taxable wages (as opposed to pre-tax deductions such as Cafeteria plans and employee 401(k) contributions).

Alien: An individual living in or visiting the United States who is not a U.S. citizen.

Americans with Disability Act (ADA): The ADA prohibits employers and employment agencies from discriminating against qualified job applicants and employees with a physical or mental impairment who can, with or without reasonable accommodation, perform the essential functions of the job they would be or are doing.

Annuity: The amount withheld from salary to purchase a tax-sheltered annuity (TSA).

Automated Clearing House (ACH): A Federal Reserve Bank or other financial institution acting as a clearing house for direct deposit transactions.

Backup Withholding: Federal income tax withholding on non-employee compensation required when the payee either fails to furnish the payer with a TIN (Tax Identification Number) or when the IRS notifies the payer that the payee's TIN is incorrect.

Base Period: When dealing with unemployment compensation the "base period" usually consists of the first four quarters out of the last five completed before the claimant's benefit year.

Biweekly: Once every two weeks.

BSO: Business Services Online – an internet wage reporting service for employers provided by the Social Security Administration.

Cafeteria Plan: A plan that offers flexible benefits under IRC (Internal Revenue Code) Section 125. Each employee covered by the plan can choose from various benefits which are generally paid for with pretax deductions from the employee's wages.

Catch-up Contributions: Refers to elective deferrals by an employee to a defined retirement plan or IRA above the plan-mandated limits (for employees age 50 or over).

Circular A: IRS Publication 51, Agricultural Employer's Tax Guide. Publication 51 covers the regulations and instructions for withholding, depositing and reporting federal employment taxes for farm workers.

Circular E: IRS Publication 15, Employer's Tax Guide. Publication 15 covers the regulations and instructions for withholding, depositing and reporting federal employment taxes.

COBRA: The Consolidated Omnibus Budget Reconciliation Act of 1985. Under COBRA terminated employees have the option to continue their health insurance coverage with their former employer for a certain period of time following their termination. COBRA applies to any organization with 20 or more employees.

COD: Court Ordered Deduction. Any legal notice ordering an employer to deduct money from an employee's wages and pay that money directly to the court or to another agency (child support, garnishments, etc.).

CODA (Cash Or Deferred Arrangement): A retirement plan that allows employees to either have the employer contribute a certain amount to the plan or to receive that same amount in cash.

Combined Filing: A filing which includes tax liability and payments for more than on tax type. California for example requires combined deposits and filings for State Income Tax, State Unemployment Insurance, and State Disability Insurance.

Common Law Employee: A worker who is considered an employee because the employer has the right to direct how, where, and when the person's work will be performed, in addition to determining what work is to be done.

Common Pay Agent: Employers with multiple Federal Employer Identification Numbers (FEINs) who are allowed (under IRS rules) to consolidate their tax returns and tax payments under a single FEIN.

Common Paymaster: A situation where an employee works for two or more related companies at the same time and the related companies are treated as a single employer for employment tax purposes.

Compensatory Time: Paid time off given to an employee for working extra hours.

Constructive Receipt: "Constructive Receipt" of wages occurs when an employee's pay is available to him or her, free of any substantial limitation or restriction. **Note:** If a payroll has a pay date of say, 9-30 or 12-31 but one or more employees don't receive their check or direct deposit until after that date, then those employees' wages actually apply to the next quarter or the next year under the concept of constructive receipt.

Covered Wages: In general wages include all payments made to employees for services rendered, including salaries, bonuses, commissions, vacation allowances and many fringe benefits, regardless of what form the payment is made, when it's made or on what basis of production it's based. Wages also include the cash value of other forms of remuneration such as the reasonable value of food or lodging. Necessary business expenses reimbursed or advanced to employees such as per diem or traveling expenses are usually not considered taxable wages.

Credit reduction: Employers are not entitled to full credit for unemployment contributions made to states that have outstanding loans with the Federal Unemployment Trust Fund. Those states are referred to as "credit reduction states" and the credit percentages employers can claim for contributions made to those states are published annually in Part 1, line 6 of Form 940.

DBA: Doing Business As (the name under which an individual or business operates).

Deductions: An amount subtracted from an employee's gross pay. Deductions, other than taxes, can be taken before taxes are calculated (pre-tax deductions) or after taxes are calculated, depending on the type of deduction. Pre-tax deductions include items such as Section 125 cafeteria plan contributions.

Deferred Compensation: Benefit plans under which employees may contribute a percentage of their wages to a tax deferred savings plan (usually a 401(k) plan). Employee contributions are exempt from federal income tax and, in some states, from state income tax but are not exempt from FICA (Social Security and Medicare) withholding. Employer contributions (if any) are tax-free. Contributions and earnings accumulate until distributed to the employee, at which point the employee must pay federal income tax (and state income tax if applicable) on his or her distribution.

Defined Contribution Plan: A plan where the final retirement benefit is variable but the current contribution amount is defined (i.e., a pre-determined amount).

De Minimus Fringe Benefit: Any employer provided property or service having such a small value that accounting for it would be impractical and unreasonable, may be excluded from income as a "de minimus" fringe benefit.

Direct Deposit: Electronic transfer of an employee's net pay directly into his or her bank account in place of printing a check.

Director's Fees: Fees paid to the director of a corporation. They are not subject to Federal income tax withholding, FICA tax or FUTA tax. Director's fees are treated as self-employment income and a 1099 is issued to the director at the end of the year.

Disposable Income: The portion of an employee's earnings which is left after subtracting the deductions required by law (primarily taxes and mandatory dues).

Earned Income Credit (EIC): A tax credit available to low income employees which can be taken by the employee on his or her individual tax return. Advance EIC payments will no longer be made through payroll after December 31, 2010.

EEO-1 Report: A report filed annually with the federal government by employers with federal government contracts of $50,000 or more and 50 or more employees, or employers without government contracts but with 100 or more employees. The EEO-1 includes company data about the number of women and minority employees in specified occupational categories and subcategories. The EEOC (Equal Employment Opportunity Commission) uses the report to support enforcement of Title VII of the Civil Rights Act, which prohibits discrimination on the basis of race, color, religion or national origin.

EFT: Electronic Funds Transfer.

EFTPS: Electronic Federal Tax Payment System. An electronic system for reporting and paying federal taxes (go to www.eftps.gov for further information on enrolling and paying taxes using the EFTPS.

EIN: Employer Identification Number -- usually refers to an employer's Federal Identification Number (FEIN).

Elective deferral: A contribution to a deferred income plan such as a 401(k) plan.

Employee Leasing Company: A company that leases employees to another business on a contract basis. The leasing company handles all personnel matters and is generally considered the employer of the leased employees.

Employee Payroll Advance – Many employers will advance a certain amount of money to employee interest-free when the employee needs money quickly. The employer generally deducts a percentage from the employee's following paychecks until the advance is repaid.

Employee self-service – Allowing employees to change certain information about themselves (such as home address, marital status, or number of withholding allowances) using an online portal. Note: the same type of system can be used to let managers make changes to employee information for people in their department.

Employer's Supplemental Tax Guide: IRS Publication 15-A, which provides more detailed information than the Circular E (IRS Pub 15) regarding topics such as employee status determination, types of employee compensation, sick pay reporting, and rules for paying employment taxes.

ERISA: Employee Retirement Income Security Act of 1974 – sets protection standards for people in most private-sector retirement plans.

Escheat: The legal process involved in turning over unclaimed client checks (such as refund checks) to the state government.

ESOP: Employee stock ownership plans (ESOPs) are a type of deferred compensation plan in which the investments are primarily in employee stock.

ESPP (Employee Stock Purchase Plan): A type of employee benefit that allows participating employees to purchase company stock at a reduced price.

ETT: Employment Training Tax – a tax imposed on employers operating in California to provide funds to train employees in targeted industries in order to improve the competitiveness of California businesses.

EVS (Employment Verification Service): A free service provided by the Social Security Administration to verify the Social Security numbers of current or prospective employees. (www.ssa.gov/employer/ssnv.htm)

Excludable deductions: Deductions that are subtracted from an employee's gross earnings before a lien deduction is calculated.

Excludable earnings: Earnings that are subtracted from an employee's gross earnings before a lien deduction is calculated.

Exempt Employees: Employees who are exempt from the overtime provisions of the Fair Labor Standards Act (FLSA) because of their level of decision-making authority. In general, managers, supervisors, administrators and other in leadership roles can be classified as exempt employees.

Expatriates: U.S. citizens working in a foreign country. In general money earned by a U.S. citizen or a resident alien working anywhere in the world is subject to U.S. taxes (see https://www.irs.gov/Individuals/International-Taxpayers/Persons-Employed-Abroad-by-a-U.S.-Person for further information).

Federal Employer Identification Number (FEIN): The identification number assigned to employers by the Internal Revenue Service.

Federal information Processing Standard (FIPS) Code: The code on a child support order that identifies the agency receiving the payment.

Federal Reserve Bank: An independent agency of the U.S. government that deals with monetary policy, the regulation of financial institutions and the regulation of domestic payment systems such as Fedwire and ACH.

Federal Unemployment Tax Act (FUTA): A federal law enacted in 1939 which sets guidelines for the administration of unemployment compensation programs. All liable employers pay a federal tax to fund State and Federal unemployment insurance programs.

FICA: Federal Insurance Contributions Act (covers the combined payroll taxes for Social Security and Medicare).

FIT: Federal Income Tax.

FSA: Flexible Spending Account – an account funded by an employee through pre-tax contributions that can be used to pay for health care expenses not covered or only partially covered by the employee's medical, dental and vision insurance ($2550 limit for 2016 on annual employee contributions).

FLSA: Fair Labor Standards Act (establishes minimum wage, overtime pay, record keeping and child labor standards for almost all full and part-time workers in the United States.

FMLA: Family and Medical Leave Act. The FMLA guarantees 12 weeks unpaid leave to most employees to care for newborn or newly adopted children or to deal with a serious injury or illness to the employee or member of his or her family.

Form W-2: Employee Wage and Tax Statement.

Fringe Benefit: Cash, services or property that an employer provides to employees in addition to their regular wages. Amounts paid by the recipient for the fringe benefit are not taxable – however the value of the fringe benefits are taxable unless specifically excluded by IRS regulations. The fair market value of a non-cash fringe benefit (less any amount paid for the benefit by the recipient) is considered wages and should be included in the employee's pay and taxed accordingly.

FUTA: Federal Unemployment Tax Act.

FUTA Tax: Federal Unemployment Tax

Garnishment: A legal process that authorizes an employer to pay part of an employee's wages to a creditor to satisfy a debt owed by the employee.

Group-Term Life Insurance: Term life insurance provided to employees, paid for by the employer, the employee, or both.

HCE (Highly Compensated Employee): An employee who receives compensation in the top 20% of all employees, is at least a 5 percent owner in the business and exceeds certain annual compensation levels as defined by the IRS.

HI: Retirees' health insurance. A federal government benefit program funded by Medicare taxes.

HRIS: Human Resources Information System.

HRMS: Human Resources Management System.

HSA: Health Savings Accounts are tax-favored IRA-type trust accounts that eligible individuals - those covered by certain types of high-deductible health plans (HDHPs) - can use to pay for certain medical expenses incurred by themselves or their families. Money in the account not spent during the year stays in the account and generates tax-free interest. HSAs can be funded on a pre-tax basis through a cafeteria plan and in that case all employer contributions to the employee's account (by means of employee salary reduction) should be reported in Box 12 of the W-2 using code "W".

Imputed Income: The value of cash or non-cash employee compensation. Examples of imputed income include: dependent care assistance or adoption assistance that exceeds the tax-free amount, group term taxable life insurance coverage over $50,000, personal use of an employer-provided vehicle, and non-deductible moving expense reimbursements. Imputed income is subject to FICA withholding but not federal income tax withholding and must be reported on the employee's W-2.

IRC: Internal Revenue Code.

151

IRCA: Immigration Reform and Control Act of 1986. Prohibits employers from hiring individuals who are not authorized to work in the United States.

Independent Contractor: A non-employee contracted by a business to perform work of some type. The business species what work is to be performed but the contractor determines when, how and who will actually do the work.

IRS: Internal Revenue Service.

ISO (Incentive Stock Option): A statutory stock option that allows an employee to purchase company stock below current market price.

Key Employee – For 2016 a Key Employee as defined by the IRS, is an officer whose annual earnings are over $170,000, a 1% owner of the business with an annual earnings over $150,000, or a 5% owner in the business.

Leased Employees: Employers can lease highly skilled employees as a cost-saving measure. The leasing company hires and trains the workers and the employer pays a fee to the leasing company in return. Leased employees are usually employed on a long term basis.

Medicare: Federal hospitalization plan for U.S. citizens 65 or older, funded through Medicare tax withheld for employees' pay combined with matching amounts from employers. There is no annual wage limit for Medicare withholding.

Minimum Wage: The lowest hourly amount an employer can pay an employee under federal or state law.

MMREF (Magnetic Media Reporting and Electronic Filing) Specifications: A set of Social Security Administration specifications for filing W-2 and W-2C forms electronically.

NACHA: National Automated Clearinghouse Association.

New Hire Reporting: Required reporting of new or rehired employees to the appropriate state agency to help in collecting child care payments and in detecting abuse of the state's unemployment compensation or other assistance programs for the unemployed.

Non-cash fringe benefits: Benefits provided to employees in some form other than cash (e.g., health or life insurance) – benefits of this type may or may not be taxable.

Non-exempt Employee: Employees (hourly or salaried) who are covered by the minimum wage and overtime pay provisions of the Fair Labor Standards Act (FLSA).

OASDI: Old-age Survivor and Disability Insurance. A federal government benefit program funded by Social Security taxes.

ODFI: Originating Depository Financial Institution. A financial institution that is qualified to initiate direct deposit entries submitted by an employer.

Overtime: Hours worked in excess of the maximum set by federal or state law (generally anything over 40 hours in a given one week period).

Overtime Premium: An amount equal to one half of an employee's regular rate of pay times the number of overtime hours worked.

Partial Unemployment: Refers to a worker who is still an employee but, because of circumstances beyond his or her control, didn't work a full week and earned less than his or her normal weekly pay. Partial unemployment claims are usually filed by the employer.

Paycard: Debit cards funded by employers with the employees' net pay (can be used the same as a regular debit card).

Per diem: A daily expense payment, usually made for food or transportation.

Pieceworker: An employee who is paid per unit or number of pieces produced.

PIN: Personal Identification Number.

PIT: Personal Income Tax.

Pre-Note: A zero amount ACH transaction used to verify the accuracy of a person's bank account information before any actual transactions are processed for that person.

Pretax Deduction: A deduction from gross pay that reduces the employee's taxable wages (such as cafeteria plan or 401(k) plan deductions).

Qualified Employer: An employer who is eligible for a calculated tax rate due to having people actively employed during certain periods and having made all tax payments in a timely manner.

Qualified Plan: A benefit plan that meets IRS requirements for tax-favored treatment (such as Cafeteria health plans or 401(k) retirement plans).

Reporting Agent: Companies (not individuals) that perform payroll services (signing and filing certain tax returns and making federal tax deposits and other federal tax payments).

Resident Alien: In payroll terms, a resident alien is a person who passes either the "green card" or "substantial presence" test for determining resident status in the United States. Resident aliens are generally subject to federal income tax, Social Security and Medicare withholding taxes the same as any other employee.

Retroactive Pay: Wages paid for time worked in a previous workweek.

Sarbanes-Oxley Act: A federal law designed to provide protection for employees who report corporate and securities fraud by their employer.

SDI: State Disability Insurance.

Section 125: Section of IRS regulations that sets out rules and regulations regarding pre-tax deductions for some insurance premiums, un-reimbursed medical expenses and child/dependent care.

Self-Employment Contributions Act (SECA): Enacted in 1954, SECA authorizes the levying of Social Security and Medicare tax on the net earnings of most self-employed individuals. The basic tax rate for self-employed workers is 15.30 percent, twice that of regular employees due to the fact that employees pay one-half of FICA tax and employers pay the other half. If you are self-employed and your total annual income is $400 or more you have to file a Schedule SE and pay SECA tax on your net business income.

Severance Pay: A payment made to a terminated employee (usually an employee who has been terminated through no fault of his own).

Severance pay is normally intended to provide extra financial help for the ex-employee until he or she finds a new job and (unless specifically provided for in a contractual agreement) is at the discretion of the employer.

Shift Differential: Additional pay received by an employee for working shifts that are not as much in demand, such as evening or late night shifts.

Short term disability (STD): Short term disability pays a portion of an employee's salary if that employee becomes temporarily disabled due to illness or injury (except on-the-job injuries which are covered by workers compensation insurance). Typically STD policies provide payments for a period of 13 to 26 weeks.

Simplified Employee Pension (SEP): An Individual Retirement Account (IRA) with special provisions, available to self-employed individuals or small businesses with less than 25 employees. Employers can contribute up to 25% of an employee's compensation (not to exceed $40,000 per year).

Social Security Administration (SSA): The federal agency in charge of administering Social Security.

Split Shift: A work shift divided into two periods of time with some time (usually several hours) in between.

SSA: Social Security Administration.

Standard Industrial Classification Code (SIC): When an employer applies for a federal employer identification number (FEIN) the government also assigns the employer a classification number that identifies the type of activity engaged in by the business.

State Disability Insurance (SDI): An insurance plan sponsored by a state to provide compensation for employees who are unable to work due to injury or illness.

State Unemployment Insurance (SUI): A state fund used to pay benefits to unemployed workers. Each state's SUI fund is accumulated from quarterly taxes paid by each employer operating within that state.

STD: Short Term Disability.

SUB Plan: A SUB plan is tax exempt, Section 501 (c) (17) plan or trust established to provide severance pay to workers laid off due to a reduction in force or plant closing. SUB plan funds supplement state unemployment insurance benefits.

Supplemental Wages: Compensation received by an employee other than normal pay such as commissions or bonuses.

SUTA: State Unemployment Tax Authority.

Statutory Employees: Special groups of employees (such as full time insurance salespeople and certain homeworkers) whose wages are not subject to Federal Income Tax (FIT) withholding, but are subject to FICA (Social Security and Medicare) withholding and FUTA (Federal Unemployment Insurance) withholding.

Tax Levy: The attachment of a portion of an employee's wages (to the IRS or a state government) for payment of delinquent taxes.

Third Party Sick Pay: Payments made to employees by a third party insurer because of non job-related injury or illness.

TIN: Taxpayer Identification Number.

Tip Credit: The "tip credit" provision in the Fair Labor Standards Act and many state wage laws allows employers to pay tipped employees as little as $2.13 per hour if their base pay plus tips brings their hourly rate of pay to at least minimum wage.

Totalization Agreements: Agreements with other countries entered into by the United States to avoid dual taxation. Also known as Binational Social Security Agreements, these arrangements generally mean that if an employee working in one of these countries is subject to their social security laws, then the employee and the employer are exempt from U.S. Social Security and Medicare tax.

Uniform Base Period: A base period that starts on the same calendar date for a new or transitional claim for all claimants.

USCIS: United States Citizenship and Immigration Services.

Vesting: An ERISA guideline that stipulates that employees are entitled to their benefits from a pension fund, profit-sharing plan, or employee stock ownership plan within a specified period of time, even if they no longer work for that employer.

W-2: Federal form that shows an employee's annual wages, taxes, and other information (such as fringe benefits) that affect the person's federal , state and local income tax returns.

W-3: Transmittal form to accompany paper W-2 forms when sending them to the Social Security Administration. The W-3 includes the total wage and tax withholdings for the W-2 forms being submitted.

W-4: Employee's Withholding Exemption Certificate. The W-4 is used to record the number of exemptions an employee claims (and any additional withholding amount desired).

Wage assignment: Committing a portion of an employee's future earnings to be used for scheduled payments such as union dues or a car loan.

Withholding: Subtracting amounts from an employee's wages for taxes or garnishments. These amounts are then paid to the government or other agency to whom they are owed.

Workers Compensation: A state administered insurance covering wokers' job related injuries or illnesses. Workers compensation insurance provides the employee with a percentage of his or her regular wages while unable to work.

Appendix C – Payroll Calendar for 2017

Note 1: If any date falls on a Saturday, Sunday or Federal holiday, use the next business day.

Note 2: Deposit dates for semiweekly depositors are not listed below – use the following rule to determine deposit dates: taxes on wages paid on Wednesday, Thursday or Friday must be deposited by the following Wednesday; taxes on wages paid on Saturday, Sunday, Monday or Tuesday must be deposited by the following Friday.

January 10th: Employees who received cash tips of at least $20 in the preceding month must report them to the employer on Form 4070, Employee's Report of Tips to Employer.

January 16th: Deposit payroll taxes for December (monthly depositors).

January 31st: W-2 forms distributed to employees and 1099-MISC forms to contractors. Due date for filing W-2 forms either on paper or electronically (you must file electronically if you have 250 or more employees), and due date for filing 1099 forms if filed on paper or electronically. Form 941 filed with IRS for the 4th quarter of the previous year and annual Form 940 or 940EZ filed with IRS for the previous year. Deposit 940 taxes for the 4th quarter of the previous year (if liability is more than $100). NOTE: Fill out and attach Schedule A to Form 940 if you are a multi-state employer. Also, if you operated in a credit reduction state for 2016 you won't be able to take the full 5.4% credit for your state unemployment tax paid. According to final figures from the Department of Labor the only credit reduction state for 2016 is California Given those figures, instead of the normal 0.6% your FUTA tax rate for wages paid in California will be 1.8%. File SUTA (state unemployment) forms for the 4th quarter of the previous year and pay the SUTA tax for the 4th quarter. Employers with tipped employees (who employed more than 10 employees on a typical business day) must file the annual report for employees' tip income (Form 8027).

February 10th: Receive Form 4070 from tipped employees.

February 15th: Deposit payroll taxes for January (monthly depositors).

February 28th: File Form 8027 (Employer's Annual Information Return of Tip Income and Allocated Tips) if there is tip income to report.

March 10th: Receive Form 4070 from tipped employees.

March 15th: Deposit payroll taxes for February (monthly depositors).

March 31st: Due date for supplying 1095-C forms to employees and to the IRS for applicable large employers.

April 10th: Receive Form 4070 from tipped employees.

April 17th: Deposit payroll taxes for March (monthly depositors).

May 1st: File Form 941 for 1st quarter (May 10th if all taxes have been depositing timely, properly and in full), deposit 940 taxes if more than $100, and file SUTA (state unemployment tax) forms for 1st quarter.

May 10th: Receive Form 4070 from tipped employees.

May 16th: Deposit payroll taxes for April (monthly depositors).

June 10th: Receive Form 4070 from tipped employees.

June 15th: Deposit payroll taxes for May (monthly depositors).

July 10th: Receive Form 4070 from tipped employees.

July 17th: Deposit payroll taxes for June (monthly depositors).

July 31st: File Form 941 for 2nd quarter (August 10th if all taxes have been deposited timely, properly and in full), deposit 940 taxes if more than $100, file SUTA (state unemployment tax) forms and pay the SUI tax for the 2nd quarter.

August 10th: Receive Form 4070 from tipped employees.

August 15th: Deposit payroll taxes for July (monthly depositors).

September 10th: Receive Form 4070 from tipped employees.

September 15th: Deposit payroll taxes for August (monthly depositors).

October 2nd: File Employer Information Report EEO-1 Form EEO-1 with the U.S. Equal Employment Opportunity Commission (for employers with 100 or more employees).

October 12th: Receive Form 4070 from tipped employees.

October 17th: Deposit payroll taxes for September (monthly depositors).

October 31st: File Form 941 for 3rd quarter (November 10th if all taxes have been deposited timely, properly and in full), deposit 940 taxes if more than $100, and file SUTA (state unemployment tax) forms and pay quarterly SUTA tax.

November 10th: Receive Form 4070 from tipped employees.

November 15th: Deposit payroll taxes for October (monthly depositors).

December 10th: Receive Form 4070 from tipped employees.

December 15th: Deposit payroll taxes for November (monthly depositors).

Appendix D – 2017 SUI Wage Bases By State

(State Unemployment Insurance wage limits)

Alabama - $8,000
Alaska - $39,800
Arizona - $7,000
Arkansas - $12,000
California - $7,000
Colorado - $12,500
Connecticut - $15,000
Delaware - $18,500
District of Columbia - $9,000
Florida - $7,000
Georgia - $9.500
Hawaii - $44,000
Idaho - $37,800
Illinois - $12,960
Indiana - $9,500
Iowa - $29,300
Kansas - $14,000
Kentucky - $10,200
Louisiana - $7,700
Maine - $12,000
Maryland - $8,500
Massachusetts - $15,000
Michigan - $9,500
Minnesota - $32,000
Mississippi - $14,000
Missouri - $13,000
Montana - $31,400
Nebraska - $9,000
Nevada - $29,500
New Hampshire - $14,000
New Jersey - $33,500
New Mexico - $24,300
New York - $10,900
North Carolina - $23,100
North Dakota - $35,100
Ohio - $9,000
Oklahoma - $17,700
Oregon - $38,400
Pennsylvania - $9,750
Puerto Rico - $7,000

Rhode Island - $22,400 **
South Carolina - $14,000
South Dakota - $15,000
Tennessee - $9,000
Texas - $9,000
Utah - $33,100
Vermont - $17,300
Virginia - $8,000
Washington - $45,000
West Virginia - $12,000
Wisconsin - $14,000
Wyoming - $25,400

** Note: For approximately 75% of employers the wage base will be $20,600. For employers that pay at the highest UI rate of 9.79% (25% of employers), the wage base will be $21,700.

Appendix E – State Tax Links

Go to: www.payroll-taxes.com/state-tax for information on state withholding tax, state unemployment insurance tax, additional state taxes, and new hire reporting, as well as links to various state agencies.

Appendix F – IRS Tax Forms

1099 Forms:
- **1099-A** – Acquisition of Secured Property.
- **1099-B** – Proceeds from Broker and Barter Exchange Transactions.
- **1099-C** – Cancellation of Debt.
- **1099-CAP** – Changes in Corporate Control and Capital Structure.
- **1099-DIV** – Dividends and Distributions.
- **1099-G** – Government Payments.
- **1099-H** – Health Insurance Advance Payments.
- **1099-INT** – Interest Income.
- **1099-K** – Merchant Card and Third Party Network Payments.
- **1099-LTC** – Long Term Care Benefits.
- **1099-MISC** – Miscellaneous Income.
- **1099-OID** – Original Issue Discount.
- **1099-PATR** – Taxable Distributions from Cooperatives.
- **1099-Q** – Payments from Qualified Educational Programs.
- **1099-R** – Distributions from Pensions, Annuities, Retirement Plans, IRAs or Insurance Contracts.
- **1099-S** – Foreign Person's U.S. Source Income.
- **1099-SA** – Distributions from an HSA, Archer MSA or Medicare Advantage MSA.

Appendix G – Federal Holidays for 2017

Monday, January 2 – New Year's Day (Since Jan. 1st falls on a Sunday)
Monday, January 16 – Birthday of Martin Luther King, Jr.
Monday, February 20 – President's Day (Washington's Birthday)
Monday, May 29 – Memorial Day
Tuesday, July 4 – Independence Day
Monday, September 4 – Labor Day
Monday, October 9 – Columbus Day
Friday, November 10 – Veterans Day
Thursday, November 23 – Thanksgiving Day
Monday, Dec. 25 – Christmas Day

Appendix H – Sample Forms and Letters

Sample Letter Asking for Abatement of a Penalty:

Universal Supply Company
1000 S. Main Street Ste 100
Anywhere, USA 70000
(999) 999-9999

March 17, 2014

Department of the Treasury
Internal Revenue Service

Subject: Request to Abate Penalty

Reference:
  Notice Number: 999CG
  Date of Notice: March 3, 2014
  Employer ID: 77-1111111
  Tax Period: December 31, 2013
  Penalty Reference Code: 501

We have received IRS Notice 999CG, a proposed penalty for filing our 2013 W-2 forms on paper rather than filing them electronically. We understand that the W-2s should have been filed electronically since we had 259 W-2 forms - however we intended to file electronically (as we did in 2011 and 2012) but the paper forms were sent in by mistake. On the advice of our payroll provider we decided not to go ahead and transmit the electronic file once we realized the paper forms had been mailed.

We are requesting an abatement because there was no intent to deliberately file the forms on paper - it was a mistake and we fully intended to submit electronically (as we will again this year). We request that you please take this into account and adjust the penalty.

Thank you,

Sample Form Authorizing a Payroll Deduction:

Employee Name: _____ SSN: _____

Deduction Effective Date: _____

Payroll Deductions:
- 401(k)   % or $ _____
- 401(k) Loan $ _____
- Health Insurance $ _____
- Child Care $ _____
- Other _____ $ _____

I agree that my gross pay will be reduced by the amount of any deduction(s) indicated above. In the event of a deduction change during the year, my employer is authorized to deduct the new amount from my pay.

If a new Employee Deduction Authorization Form is not executed on or before the next year-end I agree that this form will continue to be in force for the succeeding year.

Employee Signature: _____
Date: _____

Sample Layoff Termination Letter:

Date _____

Reginald Parker-Hurst
888 Eighth Street
Anywhere, USA

Dear Reginald,

This letter confirms our discussion earlier today that you are being laid off from your employment with Acme Universal Widgets effective immediately. Unfortunately economic conditions in the industry have resulted in declining sale, forcing us to eliminate a number of job positions.

You will receive one week's severance pay for each year that you have worked here (12 weeks in your case). We will continue to provide health insurance coverage over that period. In addition you will receive payment for your accrued vacation time with your final paycheck.

You will receive the severance payment once you have signed and returned the enclosed release of claims document. You can also expect a separate benefits status letter outlining the status of your benefits upon termination, including information about your eligibility for Consolidated Omnibus Budget Reconciliation Act (COBRA) continuing group health coverage.

You will need to keep us informed of your contact information so that we can provide you with information you may need in the future such as your W-2 form.

You've been an excellent employee – if you want us to provide references for a potential employer and assist you in some other way please let us know.

Regards,

Sample Letter Providing Proof of Income:

January 14, 2015

Ronald Whistler
Universal Widgets
999 Main Street
Anywhere, USA

Mason Funsler
2nd National Bank
100 10th Street
Anywhere, USA

Re: Proof of Income for Tom Dooley III

Dear Mr. Funsler,

The purpose of this letter is to provide income verification for Tom Dooley III with regard to his application for a home mortgage through 2nd National Bank. As Human Resources Director for Universal Widgets, I can confirm that Mr. Dooley's current salary is $42,500. He also receives an annual bonus that has averaged $2,350 for the five years he has been employed by Universal Widgets. Mr. Dooley is an employee in good standing and I foresee no reason his income wouldn't continue at this level.

Enclosed is an earnings register of Mr. Dooley's earnings over the past 12 months along with a copy of his 2014 W-2 form. If I can be of further assistance please contact me at 1-800-999-9999 or by email at rwhistler@universalwidgets.com.

Sincerely,

Sample Separation Agreement and Release of Claims:

GENERAL RELEASE OF ALL CLAIMS

As consideration for the following (list here the severance pay, extended benefits, or other items you are agreeing to provide) offered to me by (business name), I release and discharge (business name), its successors, subsidiaries, employees, officers and directors (hereinafter referred to as "the Company") for all claims, liabilities, demands, and causes of actions known or unknown, fixed or contingent, which I may have or claim to have against the Company as a result of this termination and do hereby agree not to file a lawsuit to assert such claims.

This includes but is not limited to claims arising under the Age Discrimination in Employment Act or other federal, state or local laws prohibiting employment discrimination or claims growing out of any legal restrictions on the Company's right to terminate its employees.

This release does not have any effect on any claim I may have against the Company unrelated to this termination.

I have carefully read and fully understand all of the provisions of this agreement and release which sets forth the entire agreement between me and the Company, and I acknowledge that I have not relied on any representation or statement, written or oral, not set forth in this document.

Signed: _____   Date: _____
       (employee)

Signed: _____   Date: _____
       (for the Company)

Appendix I – IRS Form I-9

Section 1:

Employee Responsibilities for Section 1

Employees must provide their:

• Full legal name
◦ If the employee has two last names (family names), include both. If the employee has two first names (given names), include both.
◦ If the employee hyphenates his or her first or last names, include the hyphen (-) between the names.
◦ Include his or her middle initial, if the employee has a middle name.
• Other names used, if applicable (e.g., maiden name).
• Current address, including street name and number (no P.O. Box), city, state and ZIP code
• Date of birth
• Check mark next to the appropriate box to indicate whether they are a U.S. citizen or national, lawful permanent resident of the United States, or an alien authorized to work in the United States.
• Alien Registration/USCIS or Form I-94 Admission number and the date employment authorization expires (if applicable)
• Signature and date

Additionally, employees may provide their:

• Social Security number (This is optional unless the employer uses E-Verify and the individual has been issued a number.)
• Telephone Number
• E-mail Address

Your employee must sign the form even if a preparer or translator helps them. The preparer or translator who helps your employee must provide his or her name and address and must sign and date the certification on the form. If more than one preparer or translator is used, have the additional preparers or translators fill out the certification on additional Forms I-9 and attach the forms to the initial Form I-9.

The date your employee enters next to his or her signature should match the date the preparer/translator signed the form.

171

Employer Responsibilities for Section 1

You must:

• Review the information your employee provided in Section 1.
• Ensure that your employee provided information in all required fields. (Note: Your employees are not required to provide a Social Security number in Section 1. However, a Social Security number may be required if you use E-Verify.)
• Ensure your employee signed and dated the form.
• Ensure the Preparer/Translator section has been completed, signed, and dated if your employee used a preparer/translator.

In addition:

• You should note whether your employees indicated in Section 1 that their employment authorization will expire.

• You may need to reverify your employee's authorization when his or her employment authorization expires. You may want to remind your employees, at least 90 days before their employment authorization expires and that they will need to present a List A or List C document to show continued employment authorization for reverification purposes. Employees must present these documents on or before the date their current employment authorization expires.

• Note that the expiration date for employment authorization provided by your employee in Section 1 may or may not match the expiration date of the List A or List C document your employee presents for Section 2, Employer Review and Verification. For reverification purposes, the earlier date should be used to determine when reverification is necessary.

Section 2:

Employee Responsibilities for Section 2

Employees must present unexpired original documentation that shows the employer their identity and employment authorization. Your employees choose which documentation to present.

Employees must present:

• One selection from List A; or

• One selection from List B in combination with one selection from List C. Note:

• List A contains documents that show both identity and employment authorization
• List B documents show identity only
• List C documents show employment authorization only
In certain circumstances, your employee may present an acceptable receipt in lieu of a List A, B, or C document. Receipts only temporarily satisfy the document presentation requirement for Section 2.

Employer Responsibilities for Section 2

An employer or an authorized representative of the employer completes Section 2. Employers or their authorized representatives must physically examine the documentation presented and sign the form.

The employer or authorized representative must:

• Ensure that any document your employee presents is on the Lists of Acceptable Documents or is an acceptable receipt.
• Physically examine each document to determine if it reasonably appears to be genuine and to relate to your employee presenting it. If you determine the document does not reasonably appear to be genuine and relate to your employee, you should allow your employee to present other documentation from the List of Acceptable Documents.
• Enter your employee's Last Name, First Name and Middle Initial (if provided) from Section 1.
• Enter the document title, issuing authority, number(s) and expiration date (if any) from the original document(s) your employee presented.
• Enter the date your employee began or will begin work for pay.
• Enter the name, signature and title of the person completing Section 2, as well as the date he or she completed Section 2.
• Enter the employer's business name and address. If your company has multiple locations, use the most appropriate address that identifies the location of the employer with respect to the employee and his or her Form I-9 completion (e.g., the address where the Form I-9 is completed).
• Return the documentation presented back to your employee.

Entering Dates in Section 2

Section 2 includes two spaces that require dates. These spaces are for:

• Your employee's first day of employment (i.e., "date of hire" which means the commencement of employment of an employee for wages or other remuneration).
• The date you examined the documentation your employee presented to show identity and employment authorization.

The Date the Employee Began Employment

The date your employee began employment may be a current, past or future date. You should enter:

• A current date
  ◦ If Section 2 is completed the same day your employee begins employment for wages or other remuneration
• A past date
  ◦ If Section 2 is completed after your employee began employment for wages or other remuneration. Enter the actual date your employee began employment for wages or other remuneration.
• A future date
  ◦ If Section 2 is completed after the employee accepts the job offer but before he or she will begin employment for wages or other remuneration, enter the date the employee expects to begin such employment. If the employee begins employment on a different date, cross out the expected start date and write in the correct start date. Date and initial the correction.

Federal contractors completing Form I-9 for existing employees as a result of an award of a federal contract with the FAR E-Verify clause:

• Enter the date their employees first began employment for wages or other remuneration from Section 2 of their previously completed Form I-9.

The Date the Employer Examined the Employee's Documents

This date is the actual date you complete Section 2 by examining the documentation your employee presents and signing the certification.

Section 3:

Employers may complete Section 3 when:

• Your employee's employment authorization or documentation of employment authorization has expired ("reverification").

174

• Your employee is rehired within three years of the date that Form I-9 was originally completed.
• Your employee changes his or her name.

Reverification

When your employee's employment authorization or employment authorization documentation (in most cases—see below for more information) expires, you must reverify to ensure your employee is still authorized to work. Look in Section 1 for the date that employment authorization expires and in Section 2 for the date that employment authorization document expires.

The employment authorization expiration date provided by your employee in Section 1 may not match with the document expiration date recorded by you under List A or List C in Section 2. For reverification purposes, the earlier date should be used to determine when reverification is necessary.

We suggest that you remind employees, at least 90 days before the date reverification is required, that your employees will be required to present a List A or List C document (or acceptable receipt) showing continued employment authorization on the date that their employment authorization or documentation expires. If your employee has a Form I-765, Application for Employment Authorization, pending with USCIS, and the application has been pending for 75 days, your employee may call the National Customer Service Center or schedule an INFOPASS appointment at a local office to request expedited processing.

Employers should not reverify:

• U.S. citizens
• Lawful permanent residents (LPRs) who presented a Permanent Resident Card (Form I-551) for Section 2
• List B documents
Unless reverification does not apply (as stated above), when your employee's employment authorization or employment authorization documentation expires your employee must present unexpired documentation from either List A or List C showing he or she is still authorized to work.

To complete Section 3, you must:

• Examine the documentation to determine if it appears to be genuine and to relate to your employee presenting it. If you feel the document does not reasonably appear to be genuine and relate to your employee, you should allow your employee to present other documentation from the List of Acceptable Documents.
• Record the document title, document number and expiration date, if any.
• Sign and date Section 3.

If you previously completed Section 3, or if the version of the form you used for a previous verification is no longer valid, you must complete Section 3 of a new Form I-9 using the most current version and attach it to the previously completed Form I-9.

Appendix J - 2017 Federal Withholding Tax Tables

Withholding Allowance Amounts:

Payroll Period	Withholding Allowance
Weekly	$ 77.90
Biweekly	155.80
Semimonthly	168.80
Monthly	337.50
Quarterly	1,012.50
Semiannually	2,025.00
Annually	4,050.00
Daily (or miscellaneous)	15.60

To figure the federal income tax to be withheld, multiply the number of withholding allowances claimed by the employee times the appropriate amount from the table above. Subtract that amount from the employee's gross pay for the pay period to get the taxable gross. Then go to the appropriate table on the following pages (based on the pay frequency - weekly, semimonthly, etc.), and look in the single or married column depending on the person's marital status. Find the wage bracket that matches the taxable gross and calculate the federal withholding tax. Note: If the employee has tax-deferred deduction amounts such as cafeteria plan deductions or 401(k) deductions, those amounts must also be subtracted from the employee's gross pay to arrive at the taxable gross.

(For Wages Paid in 2017)

TABLE 1—WEEKLY Payroll Period

(a) SINGLE person (including head of household)—

If the amount of wages (after subtracting withholding allowances) is: Not over $44 .... $0 — The amount of income tax to withhold is: $0

Over—	But not over—	The amount of income tax to withhold is:	of excess over—
$44	—$224	$0.00 plus 10%	—$44
$224	—$774	$18.00 plus 15%	—$224
$774	—$1,812	$100.50 plus 25%	—$774
$1,812	—$3,730	$360.00 plus 28%	—$1,812
$3,730	—$8,058	$897.04 plus 33%	—$3,730
$8,058	—$8,090	$2,325.28 plus 35%	—$8,058
$8,090	....	$2,336.48 plus 39.6%	—$8,090

(b) MARRIED person—

If the amount of wages (after subtracting withholding allowances) is: Not over $166 .... $0 — The amount of income tax to withhold is: $0

Over—	But not over—	The amount of income tax to withhold is:	of excess over—
$166	—$525	$0.00 plus 10%	—$166
$525	—$1,626	$35.90 plus 15%	—$525
$1,626	—$3,111	$201.05 plus 25%	—$1,626
$3,111	—$4,654	$572.30 plus 28%	—$3,111
$4,654	—$8,180	$1,004.34 plus 33%	—$4,654
$8,180	—$9,218	$2,167.92 plus 35%	—$8,180
$9,218	....	$2,531.22 plus 39.6%	—$9,218

TABLE 2—BIWEEKLY Payroll Period

(a) SINGLE person (including head of household)—

If the amount of wages (after subtracting withholding allowances) is: Not over $88 .... $0 — The amount of income tax to withhold is: $0

Over—	But not over—	The amount of income tax to withhold is:	of excess over—
$88	—$447	$0.00 plus 10%	—$88
$447	—$1,548	$35.90 plus 15%	—$447
$1,548	—$3,623	$201.05 plus 25%	—$1,548
$3,623	—$7,460	$719.80 plus 28%	—$3,623
$7,460	—$16,115	$1,794.16 plus 33%	—$7,460
$16,115	—$16,181	$4,650.31 plus 35%	—$16,115
$16,181	....	$4,673.41 plus 39.6%	—$16,181

(b) MARRIED person—

If the amount of wages (after subtracting withholding allowances) is: Not over $333 .... $0 — The amount of income tax to withhold is: $0

Over—	But not over—	The amount of income tax to withhold is:	of excess over—
$333	—$1,050	$0.00 plus 10%	—$333
$1,050	—$3,252	$71.70 plus 15%	—$1,050
$3,252	—$6,221	$402.00 plus 25%	—$3,252
$6,221	—$9,308	$1,144.25 plus 28%	—$6,221
$9,308	—$16,360	$2,008.61 plus 33%	—$9,308
$16,360	—$18,437	$4,335.77 plus 35%	—$16,360
$18,437	....	$5,062.72 plus 39.6%	—$18,437

TABLE 3—SEMIMONTHLY Payroll Period

(a) SINGLE person (including head of household)—

If the amount of wages (after subtracting withholding allowances) is: Not over $96 .... $0 — The amount of income tax to withhold is: $0

Over—	But not over—	The amount of income tax to withhold is:	of excess over—
$96	—$484	$0.00 plus 10%	—$96
$484	—$1,677	$38.80 plus 15%	—$484
$1,677	—$3,925	$217.75 plus 25%	—$1,677
$3,925	—$8,081	$779.75 plus 28%	—$3,925
$8,081	—$17,458	$1,943.43 plus 33%	—$8,081
$17,458	—$17,529	$5,037.84 plus 35%	—$17,458
$17,529	....	$5,062.69 plus 39.6%	—$17,529

(b) MARRIED person—

If the amount of wages (after subtracting withholding allowances) is: Not over $360 .... $0 — The amount of income tax to withhold is: $0

Over—	But not over—	The amount of income tax to withhold is:	of excess over—
$360	—$1,138	$0.00 plus 10%	—$360
$1,138	—$3,523	$77.80 plus 15%	—$1,138
$3,523	—$6,740	$435.55 plus 25%	—$3,523
$6,740	—$10,083	$1,239.80 plus 28%	—$6,740
$10,083	—$17,723	$2,175.84 plus 33%	—$10,083
$17,723	—$19,973	$4,697.04 plus 35%	—$17,723
$19,973	....	$5,484.54 plus 39.6%	—$19,973

TABLE 4—MONTHLY Payroll Period

(a) SINGLE person (including head of household)—

If the amount of wages (after subtracting withholding allowances) is: Not over $192 .... $0 — The amount of income tax to withhold is: $0

Over—	But not over—	The amount of income tax to withhold is:	of excess over—
$192	—$969	$0.00 plus 10%	—$192
$969	—$3,354	$77.70 plus 15%	—$969
$3,354	—$7,850	$435.45 plus 25%	—$3,354
$7,850	—$16,163	$1,559.45 plus 28%	—$7,850
$16,163	—$34,917	$3,887.09 plus 33%	—$16,163
$34,917	—$35,058	$10,075.91 plus 35%	—$34,917
$35,058	....	$10,125.26 plus 39.6%	—$35,058

(b) MARRIED person—

If the amount of wages (after subtracting withholding allowances) is: Not over $721 .... $0 — The amount of income tax to withhold is: $0

Over—	But not over—	The amount of income tax to withhold is:	of excess over—
$721	—$2,275	$0.00 plus 10%	—$721
$2,275	—$7,046	$155.40 plus 15%	—$2,275
$7,046	—$13,479	$871.05 plus 25%	—$7,046
$13,479	—$20,167	$2,479.30 plus 28%	—$13,479
$20,167	—$35,446	$4,351.94 plus 33%	—$20,167
$35,446	—$39,946	$9,394.01 plus 35%	—$35,446
$39,946	....	$10,969.01 plus 39.6%	—$39,946

Percentage Method Tables for Income Tax Withholding (continued)

(For Wages Paid in 2017)

TABLE 5—QUARTERLY Payroll Period

(a) SINGLE person (including head of household)—				(b) MARRIED person—			
If the amount of wages (after subtracting withholding allowances) is:		The amount of income tax to withhold is:		If the amount of wages (after subtracting withholding allowances) is:		The amount of income tax to withhold is:	
Not over $575 .... $0				Not over $2,163 .... $0			
Over—	But not over—		of excess over—	Over—	But not over—		of excess over—
$575	—$2,906	$0.00 plus 10%	—$575	$2,163	—$6,825	$0.00 plus 10%	—$2,163
$2,906	—$10,063	$233.10 plus 15%	—$2,906	$6,825	—$21,138	$466.20 plus 15%	—$6,825
$10,063	—$23,550	$1,306.65 plus 25%	—$10,063	$21,138	—$40,438	$2,613.15 plus 25%	—$21,138
$23,550	—$48,488	$4,678.40 plus 28%	—$23,550	$40,438	—$60,500	$7,438.15 plus 28%	—$40,438
$48,488	—$104,750	$11,661.04 plus 33%	—$48,488	$60,500	—$106,338	$13,055.51 plus 33%	—$60,500
$104,750	—$105,175	$30,227.50 plus 35%	—$104,750	$106,338	—$119,838	$28,182.05 plus 35%	—$106,338
$105,175	....	$30,376.25 plus 39.6%	—$105,175	$119,838	....	$32,907.05 plus 39.6%	—$119,838

TABLE 6—SEMIANNUAL Payroll Period

(a) SINGLE person (including head of household)—				(b) MARRIED person—			
If the amount of wages (after subtracting withholding allowances) is:		The amount of income tax to withhold is:		If the amount of wages (after subtracting withholding allowances) is:		The amount of income tax to withhold is:	
Not over $1,150 .... $0				Not over $4,325 .... $0			
Over—	But not over—		of excess over—	Over—	But not over—		of excess over—
$1,150	—$5,813	$0.00 plus 10%	—$1,150	$4,325	—$13,650	$0.00 plus 10%	—$4,325
$5,813	—$20,125	$466.30 plus 15%	—$5,813	$13,650	—$42,275	$932.50 plus 15%	—$13,650
$20,125	—$47,100	$2,613.10 plus 25%	—$20,125	$42,275	—$80,875	$5,226.25 plus 25%	—$42,275
$47,100	—$96,975	$9,356.85 plus 28%	—$47,100	$80,875	—$121,000	$14,876.25 plus 28%	—$80,875
$96,975	—$209,500	$23,321.85 plus 33%	—$96,975	$121,000	—$212,675	$26,111.25 plus 33%	—$121,000
$209,500	—$210,350	$60,455.10 plus 35%	—$209,500	$212,675	—$239,675	$56,364.00 plus 35%	—$212,675
$210,350	....	$60,752.60 plus 39.6%	—$210,350	$239,675	....	$65,814.00 plus 39.6%	—$239,675

TABLE 7—ANNUAL Payroll Period

(a) SINGLE person (including head of household)—				(b) MARRIED person—			
If the amount of wages (after subtracting withholding allowances) is:		The amount of income tax to withhold is:		If the amount of wages (after subtracting withholding allowances) is:		The amount of income tax to withhold is:	
Not over $2,300 .... $0				Not over $8,650 .... $0			
Over—	But not over—		of excess over—	Over—	But not over—		of excess over—
$2,300	—$11,625	$0.00 plus 10%	—$2,300	$8,650	—$27,300	$0.00 plus 10%	—$8,650
$11,625	—$40,250	$932.50 plus 15%	—$11,625	$27,300	—$84,550	$1,865.00 plus 15%	—$27,300
$40,250	—$94,200	$5,226.25 plus 25%	—$40,250	$84,550	—$161,750	$10,452.50 plus 25%	—$84,550
$94,200	—$193,950	$18,713.75 plus 28%	—$94,200	$161,750	—$242,000	$29,752.50 plus 28%	—$161,750
$193,950	—$419,000	$46,543.75 plus 33%	—$193,950	$242,000	—$425,350	$52,222.50 plus 33%	—$242,000
$419,000	—$420,700	$120,910.25 plus 35%	—$419,000	$425,350	—$479,350	$112,728.00 plus 35%	—$425,350
$420,700	....	$121,505.25 plus 39.6%	—$420,700	$479,350	....	$131,628.00 plus 39.6%	—$479,350

TABLE 8—DAILY or MISCELLANEOUS Payroll Period

(a) SINGLE person (including head of household)—				(b) MARRIED person—			
If the amount of wages (after subtracting withholding allowances) divided by the number of days in the payroll period is:		The amount of income tax to withhold per day is:		If the amount of wages (after subtracting withholding allowances) divided by the number of days in the payroll period is:		The amount of income tax to withhold per day is:	
Not over $8.80 .... $0				Not over $33.30 .... $0			
Over—	But not over—		of excess over—	Over—	But not over—		of excess over—
$8.80	—$44.70	$0.00 plus 10%	—$8.80	$33.30	—$105.00	$0.00 plus 10%	—$33.30
$44.70	—$154.80	$3.59 plus 15%	—$44.70	$105.00	—$325.20	$7.17 plus 15%	—$105.00
$154.80	—$362.30	$20.11 plus 25%	—$154.80	$325.20	—$622.10	$40.20 plus 25%	—$325.20
$362.30	—$746.00	$71.99 plus 28%	—$362.30	$622.10	—$930.80	$114.43 plus 28%	—$622.10
$746.00	—$1,611.50	$179.43 plus 33%	—$746.00	$930.80	—$1,636.00	$200.87 plus 33%	—$930.80
$1,611.50	—$1,618.10	$465.05 plus 35%	—$1,611.50	$1,636.00	—$1,843.70	$433.59 plus 35%	—$1,636.00
$1,618.10	....	$467.36 plus 39.6%	—$1,618.10	$1,843.70	....	$506.29 plus 39.6%	—$1,843.70

Appendix K - Notes

(Add your own notes on the following blank pages)

Alphabetical Index

76556023R00104

Made in the USA
Middletown, DE
13 June 2018